Casemate Sho

AMPHIBIOUS WARFARE

Oscar E. Gilbert and Romain V. Cansière

CASEMATE
Oxford & Philadelphia

For Catherine and Caroline

Published in Great Britain and
the United States of America in 2018 by
CASEMATE PUBLISHERS
The Old Music Hall, 106–108 Cowley Road, Oxford OX4 1JE, UK
1950 Lawrence Road, Havertown, PA 19083, USA

Paperback Edition: ISBN 978-1-61200-615-4
Digital Edition: ISBN 978-1-61200-616-1 (epub)

A CIP record for this book is available from the British Library

Printed in the Czech Republic by FINIDR, s.r.o.

Typeset in India by Versatile PreMedia Services. www.versatilepremedia.com

For a complete list of Casemate titles, please contact:

CASEMATE PUBLISHERS (UK)
Telephone (01865) 241249
Email: casemate-uk@casematepublishers.co.uk
www.casematepublishers.co.uk

CASEMATE PUBLISHERS (US)
Telephone (610) 853-9131
Fax (610) 853-9146
Email: casemate@casematepublishers.com
www.casematepublishers.com

CONTENTS

INTRODUCTION

"The difference between a river crossing, however wide, and a landing from the ocean is that the failure of a river crossing is a reverse while the failure of a landing operation is a catastrophe … My military education and experience in the First World War has all been based on roads, rivers and railroads. During the last two years, however, I've been acquiring an education based on oceans and I've had to learn all over again. Prior to the present war I never heard of any landing craft except a rubber boat. Now I think about little else."

General George C. Marshall, Chief of Staff, US Army, 1939–1945

Amphibious operations originated in prehistoric times because water transportation—be it by canoes or ships—is more efficient for moving men and supplies (or captives and loot). In modern times amphibious landings have with good reason been called the most complex of military undertakings. They require coordination between land, naval, and air forces. In land combat forces can retreat if things go wrong. In an amphibious operation it is virtually impossible to extract the landing force without catastrophic losses.

To add to the complexity, and risk, the logistics of an amphibious operation are inordinately complex. The attackers must foresee needs, and bring everything required for the operation.

In the ancient world necessary support included spare weapons and armorers, and horses. The support most often overlooked by historians is one all too familiar to modern logisticians: fuel. Horses in particular cannot simply live off of local forage, but require allocations of grain and other feed not always locally available. In the modern era requirements include not only fuel and other vehicle support systems like repair shops, but water systems, waste disposal, food preparation, hospital services, jails for prisoners, heavy construction equipment, and a host of other requirements. A large amphibious operation might best be compared to relocating an entire city.

The first real heyday of amphibious warfare came with the European colonial wars. This new era began with the global Seven Years War of 1756–1763, and reached its climax in the American War of Independence (1775–1782) and the War of 1812 (1812–1814).

Most early amphibious operations were extemporized, and sometimes resulted in botched landings that failed to achieve even local goals (Sullivan's Island/Charleston, June 1776) or outright disasters (Marathon, 490 BC). The British landings at Aboukir Bay in Egypt (March 1801) during the Napoleonic Wars saw the first example of the application of "modern" amphibious tactics, but with the immediate death of the general who formulated them, the lessons were immediately forgotten by mentally ossified generals. In the immediate aftermath of the Napoleonic Wars a very simplistic *amphibious doctrine* began to emerge.

The next great era of amphibious warfare was World War I (1914–1918), but the failure of the Gallipoli campaign (1915–1916) led analysts to conclude that massed firepower had rendered

Doctrine is best defined as a set of governing principles by which military operations are conducted to accomplish specific goals. Early doctrine held that usually the success or failure of an amphibious operation lies in factors listed by Antoine-Henri de Jomini (Général en Chef, Napoléon Bonaparte's aide-de-camp) in 1838: rapidity of execution, duping the enemy as to the landing area, topography and hydrography favorable to the attacker, adequate naval gunfire support, artillery support landed as early as possible, and capture of heights dominating the landing beaches.

amphibious attacks impossible. However, for the two powers vying for control in the Pacific Ocean, Japan and the United States, the need for amphibious operations was obvious. In the 1930s a modern and detailed amphibious doctrine appeared.

In 1940, conquest of mainland Europe by Nazi Germany threw all of the carefully crafted Allied plans for a conventional war in Europe out the window. Then in early 1942 the rapid expansion of Imperial Japan made amphibious campaigns an absolute necessity. Allied amphibious campaigns proved critical to expelling the Germans from North Africa, forcing entries into France and Italy, the recapture of southeast Asia, and the reconquest of the numerous Pacific islands.

We will trace the history and evolution of amphibious warfare from the Bronze Age until today, but any discussion of amphibious operations requires an understanding of basic terminology.

An *amphibious operation* is a military operation launched from the sea with the primary purpose of placing a landing force ashore.

An *amphibious raid* is a temporary incursion, with a preplanned withdrawal. In the modern era they are most often used to gather intelligence (Bruneval, February 1942), confuse or divert enemy attention (Makin Island, August 1942), to destroy enemy resources or key facilities (St. Nazaire, March 1942), and sometimes simply to test doctrine (Dieppe, August 1942). Raiding is an effective means to allow a weaker force or nation to boost morale, and to harass, distract, and cause dispersion of effort by a stronger enemy. These operations can have strategic results far out of proportion to the damage inflicted (Whitehaven, April 1778). In the era of European colonialism such landings were nearly ubiquitous.

An *amphibious demonstration* is a show of force with no intent to undertake an actual amphibious attack, encouraging the enemy to concentrate resources in an unfavorable location. Examples are the false landings in southern France used to divert German attention from the actual invasion sites in June 1944, and the threat posed by the American 4th Marine Expeditionary Brigade during Operation *Desert Storm* that pinned major Iraqi forces in place (January–February 1991). A less obvious example was the creation of a phantom amphibious army under George Patton, intended to make the German Army divert resources away from the Normandy coast (March–June 1944).

The *amphibious assault* involves the seizure and holding of a foothold on a defended shore. Modern doctrine for amphibious assault was originally formulated for the capture of islands to serve as advanced naval or air bases (Tarawa, 1943). The concept was of necessity expanded to include establishment of a major lodgment or the capture of a major port to allow the introduction of conventional forces for a land campaign (Normandy, June 1944). An important aspect is that the transport vessels that support the landing are *combat loaded*, i.e. the matériel likely to be needed first is loaded in the more easily accessible upper parts of the ships' cargo spaces.

An *amphibious withdrawal* is the extraction of a military force, often under threat of enemy attack. It requires a shrinking land force to maintain a beachhead against increasingly superior enemy forces (Dunkirk, May–June 1940; Hungnam, Korea, December 1950).

Though not strictly amphibious by definition, *riverine operations* are waterborne operations in environments like lakes or major rivers (Viking raids into Eastern Europe; Plains of Abraham, September 1759).

Non-combat amphibious operations include *administrative landings* where little or no opposition is expected. Vessels are *administratively loaded* to maximize use of cargo space. *Humanitarian assistance* and *crisis response* have become increasingly common and major missions of amphibious forces (Bangladesh cyclone relief, May 1991; Operation *Restore Hope*, Somalia, December 1992). Providing rapid response for the evacuation of civilians threatened by war, civil unrest, or natural disasters is a major task of the American Marine expeditionary units aboard ships in the major ocean areas (Lebanon, June–July 1976 and July–August 2006; Liberia, April–August 1996, and June 2003).

Modern amphibious doctrine was formulated by the US Marine Corps in the early 20th century, at the prodding of the US Navy, for the seizure of advanced bases in the Pacific. It was refined by exhaustive study of the reasons why the Gallipoli campaign failed.

Of other nations, only Japan paid significant attention to the need for amphibious warfare, but did not formulate a coherent doctrine. The British devoted minimal attention to the need for amphibious operations, while others, like the Germans, simply ignored the problem. Isolated behind its Atlantic and Pacific moats, US Army strategic doctrine was for administrative landings at foreign ports. When the Nazis overran most of Europe, all these carefully formulated plans went onto the trash heap of history. Amphibious warfare became the most important aspect of the Allied victory over the Axis Powers, more so than the new doctrines of armored warfare, aerial bombardment, or even weapons like the atomic bomb. The Allies simply could not bring Italy, Japan, or Germany under attack until they had first gained advanced bases or forced an entry onto landmasses by amphibious assault.

In the following chapters we will examine the causes for the success or failure of selected operations. As the history of warfare in general moved into the mid-20th century and later, the time lines of overlapping operations in far-flung parts of the world become inter-tangled. The premier example is how the amphibious landings in Normandy (June 6, 1944) completely overshadowed the Saipan (June 15) and Tinian (July 24) landings of arguably equal strategic importance.

Another issue is the sheer number of amphibious operations in World War II. It was an amphibious war, and to cover all the operations by all the combatant nations would require many hundreds of pages. For this reason not all amphibious operations of that period are covered in detail.

1194 BC	The Greeks launch the first recorded amphibious expedition against Troy.
693 BC	Neo-Assyrian king Sennacherib conducts the first known amphibious assault landing against the Elamite city state.
490 BC	A huge Persian amphibious landing is defeated at Marathon, preserving European civilization.
490–489 BC	Julius Caesar successfully invades Britain.
1066	William the Conqueror conquers Anglo-Saxon England after an amphibious landing.
1281	The Mongols achieve some success at invading Japan, only to have the invasion fleet wrecked by a "divine wind"—a *kamikaze*.
1759	A British landing climaxes with a battle on the Plains of Abraham in Canada, breaking French colonial power in the Americas.
1776	A small raid on Nassau in the Bahamas marks the inauspicious combat debut of the new American Marine Corps.
1776	A pinprick American raid on Whitehaven in northwest England outrages the British public. It is the first act in a series that will eventually turn the public and parliament against the war to suppress the American colonial rebellion.
1801	General Sir Ralph Abercromby conducts the first modern amphibious assault at Aboukir Bay, Egypt. Though successful, Abercromby's death shortly afterward assures that all his innovative ideas will be forgotten for half a century.
1815	The disastrous failure of a British amphibious campaign against New Orleans in Louisiana guarantees the unhindered westward expansion of the young United States.

1847   An American expedition against Vera Cruz in Mexico both provides experience in operating far from fixed bases, and the first use of small steam-powered vessels in amphibious warfare.

1854   The disastrous Crimean invasion demonstrates that Britain has allowed its amphibious expertise to lapse.

1861–1865   The American Civil War sees the widespread use of riverine warfare, and Union control of the seas allows decisive amphibious campaigns.

1879   The Chilean landing at Pisagua is the decisive event in the War of the Pacific, the longest and bloodiest war in South American history.

1898   The Spanish-American War marks the debut of the US Marine Corps as a true expeditionary force, and America acquires Pacific colonies that will ultimately bring it into conflict with Imperial Japan.

1914   The United States launches its first full-scale campaign against a foreign objective, Vera Cruz in Mexico.

1915–1918   Although successful British amphibious raids are conducted against German-held port facilities along the European coastline, the disastrous Gallipoli campaign (1915–1916) leads to false conclusions that will stall the evolution of amphibious warfare for decades.

1920–1939   Despite general apathy, visionaries— primarily in the United States and Japan— continue to develop amphibious doctrine and equipment.

April 1940   As World War II erupts, the Norway campaign is the first campaign on the Western Front. It conclusively demonstrates that neither the Axis nor the Allies are prepared for amphibious warfare.

May–September 1940   The British use a hastily arranged amphibious evacuation to salvage what is left of their army in France.

May–June 1941   The Germans launch a nearly disastrous airborne-amphibious invasion of Crete.

July–December 1941   The Germans and Soviets fight a number of amphibious battles from the Baltic to the Black Sea. The successful Soviet campaign to halt the German offensive against Murmansk preserves a supply line for delivery of war supplies from America and Britain.

December 1941–May 1942   The Japanese use amphibious landings to conduct a lightning conquest that reaches from the Indian Ocean to the Central Pacific. Notable events are near failure at Wake Island (December), the ill-managed invasion of the Philippines (December 1941–May 1942), and the first successful joint airborne-amphibious invasion at Timor (February 1942).

August 1942   After a major naval victory at Midway in June, the United States begins to blunt and then roll back Japanese gains, beginning at Guadalcanal.

August 1942   The British conduct a raid, actually a full-scale amphibious assault rehearsal, at Dieppe, France. It proves a total disaster.

November 1942   Landings in northwest Africa, largely American, open a new front against Rommel's forces in the desert.

June 1943   American General Douglas MacArthur commences a masterful amphibious campaign to neutralize Japanese strength in the Southwest Pacific.

July 1943   British and American forces invade Sicily, the first step in an Allied assault on southern Europe. George Patton, better known for armored tactics, skillfully uses tactical landings to outflank successive German defensive lines.

November 1943   The Americans launch the first full-scale assault on a heavily fortified beach at Tarawa. In a vicious three-day battle the Americans prevail by sheer tenacity after near disaster.

January 1944   Following a successful invasion of Italy in September 1943 the Allied offensive bogs down in mountainous terrain. Landings at Anzio are intended to outflank German defenses, but instead the Allies are penned into a small beachhead when the landing force fails to quickly capture surrounding high ground.

June 1944   After a successful deception operation results in the German defenders concentrating in the Pas-de-Calais, the Allies stage the largest airborne-amphibious assault in history in Normandy.

February 1944–March 1945   The Central Pacific drive toward Japan is conducted along doctrinal lines defined in the 1920s, with the conquest of a series of objectives for use as naval and air bases. The climactic event is the February–March 1945 battle for Iwo Jima.

April–June 1945   American strategy has changed, and the two major Pacific amphibious drives converge at Okinawa instead of Formosa.

August 1945   The dropping of the atomic bombs eliminates the need for Operation *Downfall*, planned as the largest amphibious assault in history on two of the Japanese Home Islands, operations *Olympic* and *Coronet*.

October 1949   The climactic event of the Chinese Civil War is the invasion of Hainan, but several offshore islands remain in the hands of anti-communist forces until today.

September 1950   North Korean forces nearly drive South Korean and American forces off the peninsula, but an American landing at

Inchon severs North Korean supply lines and changes the course of the war.

December 1950   After China enters the Korean War, major United Nations forces are encircled in northeastern Korea. They are saved by another of the most successful evacuations in history.

October–November 1956   After Egyptian strongman Gamal Nasser seizes the Suez Canal, British, French, and Israeli forces invade Egypt. British landings at Port Said are the first significant use of helicopters in an assault from the sea.

1965–1972   The United States makes limited use of amphibious coastal raids in the Vietnam War, and more extensive use of riverine landings in the Mekong Delta region.

1974   The Turkish invasion of Cyprus is one of the least known, but most audacious and strategically successful amphibious invasions in history.

April–June 1982   When Argentina seizes the Falkland Islands, Britain is completely unprepared for a long-range amphibious campaign. A cobbled-together fleet suffers heavy losses. The result is another prediction that amphibious operations are a thing of the past.

February 1991   In Operation *Desert Storm* the threat of an amphibious landing fixes about 40 percent of Iraqi forces in place, preventing them from participating in the land battle.

November 2001   Initial Coalition operations in land-locked Afghanistan are conducted by special operations forces, but insertion of a major conventional force requires seizure of an airbase. The task is accomplished by a helicopter airlift of American Marines from ships in the Indian Ocean.

CHAPTER 1

~~~~~~~~~~~~~~~~~~~~~~~~~~~~~~~~~~

AMPHIBIOUS OPERATIONS IN ANTIQUITY

"On each flank the Athenians and Plataeans were victorious, and as they conquered, they let escape the part of the barbarian army they had defeated, and, joining their two flanks together, they fought the Persians who had broken their center; and the Athenians won the day. As the Persians fled, the Greeks followed, hacking at them, until they drove them into the sea. The Greeks called for fire and laid hold of the ships."

Herodotus, *The History*

The earliest known amphibious campaign was the Achaean and Mycenaean expedition against Troy in 1194–1184 BC. The Greeks transported an army from southwestern Greece to besiege Troy, located in what is now northwestern Turkey. The landing was essentially unopposed, and commenced a ten-year-long conventional siege.

Less well known is the world's first true amphibious assault. Elam was a small empire that encompassed much of what is now southern Iran, along the northern shore of the Persian Gulf. The Elamites were a minor annoyance to Sennacherib, ruler of the neo-Assyrian Empire from 740 to 681 BC, as he dealt with a series of rebellions in an empire that stretched from the eastern Mediterranean to the Persian Gulf. The Elamites encouraged these rebellions, so in 694 BC Sennacherib decided to put an end to them. He assembled a fleet of boats built and manned by the master boat-builders of

Phoenicia, and moved an army down the Tigris River. Delayed by a rebellion in which the Elamites had placed a puppet king on the throne of Babylon, the army resumed the campaign against Elam in 693 BC.

Blocked by Elamite positions on the lower Tigris, the boats were moved overland to the Euphrates, and sailed down to attack the Elamite capital at the mouth of the river. "My warriors reached the quay of the harbor, like locusts they swarmed out of the boats onto the shore against them and defeated them."

Even less well known are the amphibious operations conducted by the Chinese Wu state in the extensive marshy regions at the mouth of the Yangtze River between 771 (some sources say 722) and 476 BC. Like the Greeks, the Wu and their rivals the Ch'u made extensive use of waterborne logistics to support land campaigns, but the Wu also used war canoes for riverine raids.

Marathon, 490 BC

The origins of the first Persian campaign to subdue Greece began with the support of Athens for the 499–493 BC Ionian Revolt, an attempt by ethnic Greek city states in the eastern Aegean Sea and on the western Turkish mainland to overthrow Persian rule. The Persian emperor Darius crushed the rebellion, but foresaw continued meddling of the Greeks in Persian territories.

In 490 BC he launched a major amphibious campaign against Athens. An amphibious campaign was the only real choice for Darius. The huge Persian army, numerous enough to "drink the rivers dry" simply could not feed itself from local resources no matter how ruthlessly it plundered. An even greater problem was feeding the horses, which were dependent upon masses of feed shipped by sea. The army was also dependent upon sea transport to effectively bypass the rugged terrain of eastern Greece. The spearhead troops were embarked aboard a huge fleet of 600 triremes. The fleet was further composed of some 200 or more supply carriers, and about 50 horse transports.

Darius put his force ashore on a small plain at Marathon. From Marathon he could march overland to attack Athens and its port,

Piraeus, from the weaker landward side in a conventional siege. The Marathon Plain was bounded on either side by marshes, bisected by a river, and hemmed in by mountains. The terrain was unsuitable for cavalry, the primary arm of the Persian forces, but the confined battle space was almost ideal for the Greek *hoplite* heavy infantry.

Darius made a mistake that would be replicated in other major invasions at Gallipoli (February 1915) and Anzio (January 1944). Rather than moving quickly inland, the Persians encamped for several days and failed to establish a beachhead that would give their light infantry space to outmaneuver a Greek force whom they outnumbered about 2½:1. The delay allowed the Greeks to block the exits from the small plain. The arrival of Persian cavalry would have provided shock troops to which the Athenians had no counter, and lessen the effect of the *hoplite* heavy infantry that were the centerpiece of Greek tactics.

The Greek commander Miltiades arrayed his force with a weak center (four ranks of *hoplites*) and strong flanks (eight ranks). The Greeks closed rapidly to minimize the effectiveness of the superior Persian archers, and crashed into the Persian light infantry. The Persians had some success in the center, pushing back the thin Greek line. The *hoplites* on the flanks folded inward in a double envelopment. The Persian center collapsed and ran for the shore with the Greeks in pursuit.

The disorganized Persians faced the extremely thorny problem of a retrograde shore-to-ship movement that has confounded more sophisticated armies. The Greeks pursued the fleeing enemy into the shallow water as the ships frantically backed away from the shore. The ensuing slaughter was a lopsided Greek victory. The Athenians suffered 192 dead and the Plataeans only eleven. Persian losses were seven ships captured, with 6,400 bodies counted and innumerable others drowned or concealed in the marshes where they had fled.

The Greeks had destroyed only about half of Darius's force, and the Persian fleet sailed around Cape Sounion to attack Athens from the sea. The Athenians made a forced march to forestall another landing, and rather than risk the remainder of his army in another opposed landing, Darius turned and set sail back to Asia.

Darius died, leaving his son Xerxes to attempt another invasion of Greece in 480 BC, but he was thwarted by Greek resistance at Thermopylae and suffered crippling losses in the naval battles of Artemesium and Salamis. At considerable cost the Persians succeeded in conquering Athens, but blocked at the Isthmus of Corinth, had no way to attack Sparta without a greater amphibious capability. Without adequate fleet transport to keep them supplied, the Persian army withdrew into Asia.

The strategic effects of the repulsed invasions were far-reaching. The failure of the two invasions thwarted Persian attempts to extend the empire into Europe and preserved a European culture from destruction.

ASSESSMENT: Defeat at Marathon due to failure to expand the beachhead, allowing the defenders to fight on tactically favorable terms.

Imperial Rome: The Invasion of Britain, 55 and 54 BC

As a land-based power, and operating primarily around the periphery of the Mediterranean, the Romans were always more comfortable with extended land campaigns. Oddly enough, the legions—with a reputation for sophisticated military engineering—proved less than efficient in even unopposed river crossing operations.

After some initial land battles, the First Punic War against Carthage (264–241 BC) was primarily a naval war. Unable to successfully match the traditional ramming tactics of the Carthaginian fleet, the Romans fell back on a system that took advantage of their infantry experience. The *corvus* was a folding bridge designed to allow boarding by marines, but the Roman naval infantry did not engage in any significant landing operations. The Second and Third Punic wars (218–201 BC, and 149–146 BC) were almost entirely land campaigns.

By far the most decisive Roman amphibious operations were Julius Caesar's successive invasions of southern Britain. In 55 BC Caesar launched an operation to eliminate support from Britain provided to his enemies in Gaul (France). Roman reconnaissance was inadequate with the fleet first attempting to land troops and seize a port near Dover on August 23. Driven off by superior forces on the cliffs, the fleet moved west. The Britons' cavalry and chariots were able to move overland at a speed that matched the primitive ships.

Eighty local ships pressed into service by the Romans were deep-hulled, designed for stability in heavy seas, and unsuitable for beaching. The Roman soldiers balked at plunging into the unknown water until the standard bearer of the X Legion exhorted the troops: "Leap, soldiers, unless you wish to lose your eagle to the enemy. For my part, I will do my duty to the Republic and my general." With their usual dogged determination the Roman infantry drove back the disorganized tribesmen and the Romans established a precarious beachhead.

Caesar's cavalry had sailed aboard 18 ships from a different port and were delayed by foul weather. The Romans could not exploit the successful landing but were instead penned into a small beachhead. Caesar entered into negotiations with the tribesmen, but the enemy continued to harry Roman foraging parties around the small position. Accustomed to operating in the Mediterranean, the Roman commanders were unfamiliar with storms and high tides that affected the southern coast. A storm and tidal surge wrecked much of the Roman fleet. In the end Caesar accepted promises that the tribes would later send hostages to cement a truce, and retreated to Gaul aboard ships cobbled together from the wreckage of his fleet.

The next summer Caesar crossed the Channel again, with a better plan. The fleet included ships designed as landing craft to allow better beaching. The coast was also now better known to the Romans from experience and reconnaissance.

Caesar had remedied the major failings of his first landing, an inadequate landing force and a failure to occupy a large enough beachhead. He was also the beneficiary of blind luck, as the Britons chose not to oppose the landing. With a larger force and room to maneuver, the Romans were able to defeat the less organized tribes.

ASSESSMENT: Defeat followed by victory. The first Roman invasion attempt failed because of an inadequate landing force and failure to expand the beachhead. The second succeeded when those shortcomings were remedied.

The Norman Invasion of England, 1066

There was considerable intermarriage between Normans and the older Anglo-Saxon families of England. The January 1066 death of the Anglo-Saxon king of England, Edward the Confessor, led to the placement of his brother-in-law Harold Godwinson on the English throne. A rival claimant to the throne was Duke William III of Normandy. One of William's supporters, Harald Hardrada, King of Norway, invaded northeastern England, but after initial victories was defeated at Stamford Bridge on September 25.

With Harold's forces concentrated in the north, William staged an unopposed landing in southern England on September 28. William easily brought over from Normandy a large mixed force of infantry supported by cavalry and archers, but, dependent upon supplies brought across the English Channel, did not quickly expand his beachhead.

Harold took part of his force on an exhausting march southward, gathering other forces as he went. Historians have speculated that Harold's march was so rushed because he wanted to prevent William from expanding his beachhead. With a larger and rested force, William marched to meet Harold well inland, and defeated him at Hastings on October 14.

ASSESSMENT: William succeeded because he was able to put ashore a numerically superior all-arms force unmolested, to engage an exhausted and less organized infantry force.

The Late Medieval Era, 13th–15th Centuries

The primary wars that relied upon any form of amphibious warfare were the Crusades. Of necessity the most effective campaigns made use of sea transport to move troops, horses, and supplies across the Mediterranean. In 1249 Louis IX of France launched the Seventh Crusade, an ambitious plan to conquer wealthy Egypt as a stepping stone to the Holy Land. Louis "went forth with a mighty collection of people, horsemen, and footmen, and soldiers, and mighty men of war, and they sailed on the sea in great ships and in vessels which were filled with an endless amount of gold and silver, and weapons of war, and provisions."

The first objective was Damietta, a small port north of Cairo. The savage reputation of the Crusaders preceded them, and the populace of Damietta fled the city, telling the Sultan Malik Salih, "we are afraid lest that which happened once in Akko [Acre, captured in the Third Crusade of 1191] may happen to us; the Franks killed them, and no man pleased them."

The landing was unopposed, but did not push inland. The Crusaders contented themselves with the amenities of the city, and with food supplied by the fleet. Eventually "Their contemptuous mind did not permit them to have patience until they learned the lie of the country, and the fords of the rivers, and the roads, but they made haste and crossed a canal from the Nile, and they marched a long way from water towards Egypt [Cairo] by a road where there was no water." The Muslim forces flowed along in their wake, severing the Frankish supply line, and letting the desert weaken the invaders. They defeated the Crusaders, and forced Louis to enter into a pact in which he promised peace for 120 years.

ASSESSMENT: Failure because of inadequate reconnaissance of the inland terrain, and failure to quickly move inland allowed the defenders time to concentrate forces.

The Viking Age,
Late 8th Century—Mid-11th Century AD

Although best remembered for the warlike aspects of their culture, the Scandinavians were primarily an agricultural and commercial civilization. Although most people are familiar with the so-called long ship (*langskip*), the Vikings actually constructed multiple types, including capacious cargo carriers (*knerrir*) with enclosed cargo holds, and the general purpose *knorr*.

The sturdy *langskip* was a versatile craft, capable of operating in environments as diverse as the North Atlantic and the rivers of

Eastern Europe. The wide beam, shallow draft, and absence of a prominent keel made it ideal for operating in shallow water, and beaching virtually anywhere.

Archeological evidence reveals a diverse trade, with the Vikings exporting commodities like soapstone, walrus ivory, and especially luxury furs in exchange for goods from as far away as the Arab Caliphate. Trade centers were founded in places like Kiev, and by the 11th century the Vikings were trading in goods from as far away as China and India.

One of the most lucrative trades was that of European slaves sold to the Caliphate through trading centers like Venice and Marseilles. The primary source of slaves was the famed amphibious raids, a pillar of the Viking economy. By far the greatest source of slaves was riverine raids on the Slavic settlements of Eastern Europe. Through this trade two words entered the English vocabulary, *thrall* as in enthrall, Old Norse for a slave or serf, and the word slave itself, from Latin *esclava*, a Slavic woman captive.

The age of Viking raids is best documented in the history of Ireland from the raids on the monastery at Lindisfarne in 793 through 980.

ASSESSMENT: Viking raids were successful because the greater mobility of their ships, and poor land communications, consistently permitted the element of surprise.

The Mongol Invasions of Japan, 1274 and 1281

In mid-November 1274 the emperor Kublai Khan first set his sights on the conquest of islands in the Sea of Japan. The Mongols quickly overwhelmed the defenders with a large and well-organized invasion force of 30,000 men and 900 ships, including shallow-water landing boats. In the face of fierce resistance the Mongols established small beachheads on the main island of Kyushu, but retreated to the shelter of their ships when their supply of arrows was exhausted. On the night of November 19/20 a seasonal storm wrecked the beached ships, and the Mongol survivors departed.

Though little known in the west, the second failed invasion was one of the greatest disasters in military history. The *Ise no Kami-kaze* (Divine Wind of Ise) entered Japanese mythology as a sign of divine favor and protection for Japan, a myth that would have terrible consequences in the mid-twentieth century.

In 1281 Kublai Khan mounted a second attempt, with an even larger force divided into two attack fleets. The main fleet landed first on Honshu in early June, where the landing met with fanatical resistance. The Japanese were in a period of rapid naval decline, and several days of fighting were marked by aggressive counterattacks by small Japanese boats as opposed to the larger ships of past years.

The Mongol fleet withdrew and concentrated off Takashima Island (north of modern Kyoto). At the last moment the Mongol fleet was destroyed by an unusually powerful typhoon on August 15/16. Of the total Mongol force of about 142,000 men and 3,400 ships, only about 30,000 men and 200 ships eventually returned to China and Korea. The Japanese seized the opportunity to launch an amphibious campaign to recapture the islands taken by the Mongols.

ASSESSMENT: Abject failure. Waterborne mobility to choose the point of attack, and overwhelming numbers, should have assured a Mongol victory. Dispersion of effort and a resolute beach defense, along with inadequate Mongol logistics, thwarted the landings. In both campaigns sheer luck, in the form of weather, assured Japanese victory.

The struggle between the Western European (primarily Venetian–Spanish) and Muslim alliances for control of the Mediterranean sputtered on for centuries, driven as much by competing economic interests as by religion (the Venetians in particular engaged in a thriving slave trade with the Muslim nations). The Arab aphorism that "God has given the earth to the Muslims and the sea to the Christians" pretty much sums up the imbalance that led to strategic stalemate. The climactic event was a 1564 Turkish amphibious campaign against Malta, whose defeat marked the end of Muslim attempts to extend power into the western Mediterranean, though the corsair states of northern Africa would plague commerce for several more centuries.

The struggles with Islam did not mean that the Western European powers lessened their internecine warfare. The nationalistic wars triggered by the Protestant Reformation were primarily land campaigns, but notable for the catastrophic Spanish attempt to invade England in the summer of 1588. The Spanish Armada was ill-suited to contend with the English fleet, more for reasons of unfortunate decision-making than any other reason, and the Armada was dispersed by storms, ending Spanish and Papal designs on England.

CHAPTER 2

EUROPEAN COLONIALISM AND NEW WORLDS

"I wish to have no connection with any ship that does not sail fast; for I intend to go in harm's way."

John Paul Jones

The waning days of the conflict between Western European powers with the declining Islamic powers to a great degree overlapped in time with the beginnings of European colonialism. The discovery and subjugation of the New World was of necessity a prolonged series of amphibious expeditions that bridged major oceans. The contending powers also fought a series of small wars to pluck the low-hanging fruit of each other's East Indies and Oriental colonies. Many of these ventures were conducted by private investors, and many were simply the transport of armies for land combat. The major contenders were the foes in the Anglo-Spanish War of 1585–1604. The struggle for dominance between Spain and Portugal, and rising English power, was marked by extensive privateer amphibious raiding.

The only really notable amphibious assault was the 1594–1595 attack by a private army raised by British investors under James Lancaster to capture the wealthy Portuguese colony at Recife, in easternmost Brazil. The force was transported in chartered ships, and in contrast to the usual practice of simply arming the ships' crews as landing parties, the expedition was unusually well-prepared. A galley suitable for operating in the shallow waters off the port was disassembled and carried as deck cargo aboard Lancaster's ships.

Off Recife Lancaster encountered three Dutch ships that had just loaded cargo for Europe. The Dutch captains, with the assurance that they could share in the booty from looting the city, switched sides to assist Lancaster. The reassembled galley led a contingent of ships' boats against the fort guarding the entrance to the harbor. The boats rammed themselves onto the rocks beneath the fort's guns in a do-or-die assault. The English captured and briefly held the fort and town against counterattack. They loaded a rich harvest of goods from the town's warehouses, and Lancaster even arranged to charter three hostile French ships that had arrived after capture of the town to help carry away the booty. Lancaster went on to lead the first expeditions by the East Indies Company to the East Indies and India.

The Western European nations had still not returned to the Roman practice of carrying specially trained infantry aboard warships, to serve as security (a duty normally fulfilled by the ship's master-at-arms), to provide men specially trained as boarders, and to stiffen landing parties made up of sailors untrained in land combat. At various times short-lived marine regiments had been organized, including the Spanish Infantería de Marina (1537), Portuguese Marine Corps (1610), Venetian Fanti de Mar (1622), and the French Troupes de marine (originally Troupes d'Outre-Mer, 1622). The duties of these maritime regiments were as coastal guards, naval yard security and shore battery gunners; amphibious landings were still conducted by armed sailors.

As the British grew into a global power with the fleet as its primary fighting arm, the British were the first to perceive the need for a permanent force that specialized in landing operations. The history of these naval infantry regiments was dizzyingly complex. In 1664 the British raised The Duke of York and Albany's Maritime Regiment of Foot as a fleet adjunct. Its existence was short, and it was disbanded in 1689, replaced by two army regiments, amalgamated into one in 1698. Six marine regiments and six sea service regiments were again raised in 1702 and placed directly under the command of the Lord High Admiral. Their signal accomplishment was the nearly botched amphibious assault that captured the New Mole at Gibraltar on August 1, 1704 as part of the War of the Spanish Succession. The seagoing regiments were again disbanded in 1713. By late 1739 the need for a more permanent maritime infantry force was clear, but its creation faced bureaucratic hurdles in parliament, and their existence would not be fully realized until 1755.

The Early American Experience, Mid-17th Century–Mid-18th Century

While European armies remained wedded to land campaigns and raids on each other's colonies, the virtually non-existent road systems in the New World assured that most campaigns there would of necessity be amphibious or riverine. With few regular troops stationed in North America, much of the fighting was conducted by colonial militias, raised and equipped by the chartered business interests of the English colonies, or by the stingy French and Spanish governments.

The major French base at Port Royal in Nova Scotia was a continuing thorn in the flesh of the New England colonies in disputes over lucrative fishing grounds, and as a base for French privateers. As early as 1654, the Massachusetts colony launched unsuccessful amphibious expeditions against the troublesome site, followed by defeats in 1704 and 1707, but in 1710 an expedition stiffened by 600 British Royal Marines succeeded in capturing and razing the base.

The French countered with a complex and expensive construction program for a major fortress at Louisbourg, Nova Scotia.

By 1739 the British were fighting The War of Jenkins' Ear against Spain, ostensibly over the supposed mutilation of a British merchant captain. In reality it was over control of the lucrative West Indies trade, and the boundary between British Georgia and Spanish East Florida. Operations were a mixed bag. The amphibious raid on Portolbello (modern-day Panama) of November 1739 was successful, and hailed as a great victory in London. It was followed by spectacular failures like the first attack on Cartagena (Colombia) in March 1740, and successes like the destruction of the fort at San Lorenzo el Real Chagres (Panama) in the same month. In May 1740 the British failed in another attack on Cartegena, including an amphibious assault that utilized American colonial militias. The British achieved a foothold, but were repulsed in an attack on the forts that defended the city, and then driven back into the sea. The British fleet temporarily blockaded the port, but was forced away by lack of supplies.

Expeditions against St. Augustine, Florida in 1741 and 1743 failed from poor (or no) organization. A failure at Guantanamo Bay, Cuba was followed by another repulse at nearby La Guaria in March, 1743. Clearly the British had much to learn about amphibious operations.

In 1745 an ambitious colonel of the Massachusetts Militia, William Pepperell, organized a large expedition to eliminate the French base at Louisbourg once and for all, with an unusually large and well-disciplined militia force of about 4,000 men, strengthened by British regulars. An attempted landing by colonial rangers was repulsed, but British troops were able to establish a viable beachhead west of the fortress. The Anglo-American force set about destroying French villages and fishing vessels, then occupied heights west of the fortress, allowing them to bombard it at will. The fortress had been designed to resist attack from the sea, and after a two-month siege, the French surrendered. The colonists were enraged when the British ceded the fortress back to the French in 1748, the beginnings of discord that would eventually contribute to the rupture between England and its New England colonies.

The Rochefort "Raid",
September 23 – October 1, 1757

Stung by defeats on land, the British elected to establish permanent beachheads along the French coast, and selected Rochefort as the most vulnerable target. Organizational problems bedeviled the expedition, but the British handily captured the small island of Île d'Aix and its fort that controlled the approaches to the harbor. The French were totally surprised, the defense ineffective. Despite prodding by fleet commander Edward Hawke, British general John Mourdant was indecisive and reluctant to attack the town itself. With an uncertain chain of command, Hawke felt he could not compel Mourdant to conduct the final shore-to-shore operation. As Mourdant vacillated, French reinforcements poured in. Finally Hawke gave up in frustration and withdrew his ships, forcing the landing force to withdraw.

ASSESSMENT: The British would go on to clarify doctrine and conduct more successful landings; other lessons learned were the need for adequate reconnaissance and an understanding of the overall operation by subordinate commanders. The operation highlighted a command issue that would plague amphibious operations for the next two centuries. What are the respective responsibilities of the naval and land force commanders? At what time and to what extent does the naval commander in overall charge surrender operational control to the landing force commander? And what if the army commander has seniority over the naval commander?

Quebec City, 1759

War in North America erupted again in the French and Indian Wars (1754–1763) that pitted those forces against the British colonies. In 1758 a British force, reinforced by colonial rangers, again captured Louisbourg. This time they razed it to the ground.

The decisive battle of the war, and the most significant amphibious operation, was the attack on Quebec City, the French colonial capital. The invasion force under James Wolfe was well organized, but the actual landing plan was the usual improvisation. Fortune allowed the British landing force to slip past French guns that dominated both sides of the St. Lawrence River. The French sighted a fleet of boats moving past the fortress, but assumed they were an expected convoy of reinforcements. The French had never expected a landing west of the fortress, and the northern riverbank behind the fortress was held only by weak outposts.

The British botched the landing, coming ashore at a site below steep bluffs, rather than where a road descended to the riverbank. A French-speaking officer was able to fend off verbal challenges until a sufficient force was ashore. The British were eventually able to move up the road and onto the Plains of Abraham, behind the fortress. With their plan to attack the landward side back on track, the British planned to lure the French defenders out into battle on the open plain. The French garrison commander—anticipating the arrival of a large French force advancing from the west—on September 13 obligingly sallied out to engage the British. The British, sandwiched between French forces, defeated each in detail. The fall of Quebec City was a mortal blow to French forces in North America.

ASSESSMENT: Although the British landing plan was confused and the landings botched, French negligence in not adequately defending what they believed to be an impossible landing site allowed an entire British army ashore unopposed.

When the British declared war on Spain in January 1762 they were able to make a successful landing east of Havana by use of a feint to draw Spanish defenders to the west. After a two-month siege Havana surrendered, and the British gained important bases in Florida but more importantly, Cuba.

The American Revolutionary War, 1775–1792

By the late 18th century the British were the foremost practitioners of amphibious warfare, and in general used the expertise to good effect. The famous expedition to capture rebel munitions that led to clashes at Concord and Lexington began with a covert

A British landing at The Jerseys in the American Revolution, November 1776 as depicted by British officer Thomas Davies. Note the larger boats transferring troops to smaller beaching craft, and troops climbing the trail up the cliffs. (National Archives).

shore-to-shore landing to take the rebels by surprise. In a country with poor or often non-existent roads, British naval control allowed them to move troops at will for landings anywhere along the coast, and landing parties were commonly sent ashore to capture supplies—particularly food—from coastal communities defended by local militia.

The new United States of America patterned its fleet-adjunct marines after their foes, the British Royal Marines. Observation of and experience with British amphibious campaigns in earlier times had made a considerable impression upon the colonists. As semi-isolated coastal enclaves, the New England colonies in particular rightly perceived that their future lay in maritime commerce. With the outbreak of hostilities against the mother country several of the colonies established their own navies, with "maritime militias" to serve the role of marines. In 1775 the Continental Congress approved the establishment of a small national fleet—and a corps of marines to go with it.

The creators of the new American Marine Corps faced the same conundrum as their prototype in 1740. Experienced seamen were overall more valuable to fleet operations, but could soldiers be sufficiently trained to function as adjunct sailors? Above all, how large should the force be? The ship's security contingent, a small "company" that varied with the size of the vessel, would be the basic unit, with real companies formed by combining platoons as needed. But should a regimental-scale force be organized to assist the army in land campaigns? Given the tiny scale of the new American navy and marine corps, it was a question that would not be answered for another 125 years.

George Washington organized ad-hoc detachments of naval infantry in the fighting around Boston in the summer of 1775, and other militia units participated in raids on Nova Scotia. British shore-to-shore landings on August 22, 1776 were instrumental in driving Washington's Continental Army off of Long Island. Small British amphibious raids were a constant disruption to waterborne transport in Chesapeake Bay that carried food from the Delmarva Peninsula east of the bay, "the breadbasket of the Revolution."

The New Providence (Nassau) Raid, March 3–4, 1776

The first American marines were enlisted on November 19, 1775 to fill a requirement of two battalions for an expedition against Nova Scotia. In the winter of 1776 the fleet remained icebound in the Delaware River, and by spring the strategic situation had changed. With full-scale rebellion looming, the Governor of Virginia had stores of gunpowder and small arms removed to Nassau, with plans to remove it to more defensible St. Augustine in Florida. The rebels were desperately short of gunpowder in particular, and the Continental Congress authorized a raid to recover the munitions. A fleet of eight ships carried 200 marines under Samuel Nicholas to augment the naval landing party, with Esek Hopkins as flotilla commander.

A storm scattered the fleet, and only six ships participated in the action. A plan was formulated to land from three ships at daybreak on March 3, but the force was spotted and the garrison alerted. The Americans made an unopposed landing three miles from Fort Montagu, one of the two defensive forts.

It was still a gentleman's war, and after a parlay, the British commander abandoned Fort Montagu. Hopkins neglected to blockade the harbor. While the landing party paused for the night, two British ships crept out of the harbor carrying over 80 percent of the gunpowder. The next morning the civil authorities surrendered the port.

The landing force remained ashore for two weeks, cramming the ships with the remaining arms and munitions and seizing British ships to carry the remainder. On the return voyage the fleet captured another British ship laden with arms and gunpowder, and returned to New London, Connecticut on April 8. Hopkins came under scrutiny for, among other things, not patrolling off Virginia, a secondary mission. He was forced out of the navy, but one of his subordinates, John Paul Jones, would go on to considerable fame.

ASSESSMENT: The raid failed in its primary mission through neglect to isolate the objective. Although marred by problems, it was an enormous boost to American morale, and provided expeditionary experience for the fledgling US Navy.

Sullivan's Island (Charleston), June 7–July 21, 1776

For all their expertise, British amphibious operations were not always successful. Charleston, South Carolina was one of the wealthiest cities in the colonies, one whose thriving trade was helping fund the rebellion. Landings north of the city were unopposed, but inadequate reconnaissance did not ascertain that a deep tidal creek separated the landing site from the city's main defensive fort. A shore-to-shore attempt was easily driven off by rebel riflemen. Lightened ships were able to cross a sandbar into the harbor, but bombardment of Fort Sullivan was ineffective since the sand-and-palmetto-log construction simply absorbed cannonballs. The force was driven off with heavy losses. The southern colonies remained, unmolested, in rebel hands for three more years.

ASSESSMENT: Failure due to overconfidence and inadequate reconnaissance.

The Whitehaven Raid, April 22–23, 1776

John Paul Jones had emerged unscathed from disputes that arose from the Nassau expedition, and became one of the most audacious naval officers of the war. Harassing British shipping in the Irish Sea with the USS *Ranger*, Jones decided to pay a visit to Whitehaven, where about 400 British merchant vessels packed the harbor. Jones and 30 volunteers tried to land at night from two boats, but the strong ebb tide slowed the boats and they arrived just at dawn. The landing party was able to seize the dock area but only one of the two defensive forts. Jones intended to burn the ships, but the delay had consumed most of the oil in the lanterns intended to light blazes. Only one ship was fired before the landing force withdrew.

Frustrated, Jones sailed across the bay intending to take the Earl of Selkirk or his sons prisoner in order to exchange them for American hostages, but they were not at home. Jones took the earl's silver, legal booty, which he later purchased when the prizes were auctioned, and returned it to the family.

ASSESSMENT: The raid was an abject military failure, but an outrageous political success. The British public was aghast that the rebellious colonials could land on British soil. The uproar fueled early opposition to the war, which eventually culminated in the loss of parliament's will to continue the war.

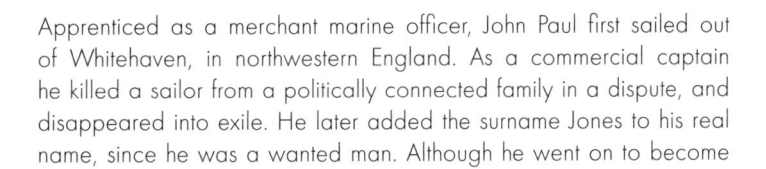

Apprenticed as a merchant marine officer, John Paul first sailed out of Whitehaven, in northwestern England. As a commercial captain he killed a sailor from a politically connected family in a dispute, and disappeared into exile. He later added the surname Jones to his real name, since he was a wanted man. Although he went on to become the "father" of both the American and Russian navies, British histories still consider him a common pirate.

Global War and the American Revolution in the South, 1778–1781

The French and Spanish smarted under the humiliating terms and loss of New World colonies that ended the Seven Years War; in late 1778 France entered the war on the side of the United States, followed by Spain. Neither was directly allied with the Americans, and French interests were directed more toward seizure of economically lucrative sugar colonies in the Caribbean. Spain's goal was the recovery of Gibraltar and East Florida. The Dutch entered the war to contest British interests in India, with a number of small amphibious campaigns.

The revolution entered its final phase with the British Southern Campaign, designed to carve off the southern colonies. British amphibious capabilities allowed them to stage operations to which the rebels could never respond in a timely fashion. It was the ability to stage amphibious operations that granted the British such successes as they were able to achieve, since land offensives from East Florida repeatedly foundered on the inability to move armies overland.

On December 29, 1778 the British forced a landing near Savannah Georgia, to which the Americans could not adequately respond since they were forced to disperse their strength along a considerable coastline. A joint Franco-American effort to recapture the city in October 1779 failed when the French fleet was unable to neutralize British fortifications. A siege ended with a failed assault on the city, the single bloodiest day of the war, with most casualties French.

A third British attempt on Charleston succeeded because the British were able to select undefended landing sites. The fall of the city on May 12, 1780 was the largest surrender of American troops until the Civil War. In the protracted struggle that followed the British were always able to fall back upon coastal enclaves for resupply and reinforcement, but were eventually forced to retreat into Virginia.

Other British campaigns were not so successful. The Anglo-Spanish War was fought primarily at sea, but Britain was overextended from

India to the Caribbean. The British governor of Jamaica hatched a plan to invade what is now Nicaragua to march across the isthmus via Lake Nicaragua, establish a connection between the Caribbean and the Pacific, and split Spain's American possessions in half. The naval commander was the young Captain Horatio Nelson, though the overall commander was Major James Polson, a captain in the regular British army.

Nelson successfully put the landing force ashore on April 9, capturing a small Spanish fort. The force of 3,000 men, mostly colonials including free blacks and Native Americans, moved up the San Juan River and laid siege to the tiny 60-man garrison at Fort San Juan. The Spanish surrendered on April 29, but by that time the landing force, ravaged by tropical diseases, had been reduced to less than 500 survivors. The landing force was withdrawn beginning on November 30.

Strategically the Spanish efforts in the Caribbean and Gulf of Mexico were better conceived, and in cooperation with the French they began systematically picking off British positions. On March 9, 1781 Spanish forces staged an unopposed landing near Pensacola, in West Florida. The fall of Pensacola on May 8 freed the French Caribbean fleet to move to the Virginia coast where Cornwallis was already surrounded on the landward side. Loss of the control of the sea to the French prevented an evacuation. The result was the October 19, 1781 surrender at Yorktown, which effectively ended British ambitions in America. The Spanish achieved the unopposed capture of Nassau in May 1782. As the American War of Independence sputtered out, Nassau was retaken by an unopposed British landing: the Spanish commander thought the invasion force were smugglers, and opposed them with customs officials.

CHAPTER 3

~~~~~~~~~~~~~~~~~~~~~~~~~~~~~~~~~~~~

THE AGE OF NAPOLEON, AND THE RISE OF NEW POWERS

"Nor must Uncle Sam's web feet be forgotten. At all the watery margins they have been present. Not only on the deep sea, the broad bay, the rapid river, but also up the narrow muddy bayou, and wherever the ground was a little damp, they have been and make their tracks."

Abraham Lincoln

With revolution and a new order in France, her interests were redirected toward European domination. The first major French overseas operation, the conquest of Egypt and Syria in the War of the Second Coalition, was directed at weakening British connections to India, increasing French trade, supporting scientific excavations of Egyptian archeological sites, and strategically outflanking France's eastern European foes.

The dominance of the British Royal Navy did not extend to success in amphibious operations. The 1797 British attempt to capture Santa Cruz de Tenerife in the Canary Islands was an unmitigated disaster. Poorly organized landings beginning on July 22 were repulsed. After the British finally achieved a lodgment and unsuccessfully attacked several forts, the landing force was compelled to withdraw.

On June 11, 1798 Napoleon landed a force on western Malta and forced the surrender of the major town, Valetta. On July 1 he landed unopposed in Egypt to begin his disastrous campaign

The failed Tenerife expedition was notable in that the commander, the ubiquitous Horatio Nelson, by then a rear-admiral, was wounded and lost an arm.

against modern-day Syria and Lebanon. The army was left isolated, its lines of supply and communication severed by the arrival of a British fleet. Most other French amphibious operations, including those on Corsica (1794), went unopposed.

Many other operations were peripheral to Europe, including the unopposed British-Russian attack on Dutch Batavia (August 1799). Much later British landings on Dutch Walcheren (July–December 1809), and British landings led to the siege of Tarragon (1813), and Krangeroen (1814).

Aboukir Bay, 1801: The First Modern Amphibious Assault

Poor army–navy cooperation resulted in a string of British disasters. General Sir Ralph Abercromby, under great political pressure, was given the task of expelling the remnants of Napoleon's army from Egypt. The mission was imperative, as Napoleon stood poised to make an alliance with Russia that would outflank the already tottering Ottoman Empire and give France complete control over the Mediterranean coast.

Abercromby worked well with his less talented naval colleague, Admiral Lord Keith, who had some experience in amphibious operations in the American Revolution. Abercromby was determined not to repeat the failures of previous operations; he began by sending intelligence agents into Egypt. Logistics are always a paramount concern, and the British faced a major problem. Drinking water would have to be supplied from ships that themselves carried little beyond the absolute minimum, so immediate capture of a viable beachhead with a water source was necessary. The British commanders first planned to land and link up with Ottoman forces at Damietta. They were dismayed to learn that their ally's army was an unreliable herd that lacked any organization at all.

Abercromby and Keith devised a plan to land at Aboukir Bay, east of Alexandria. Abercromby's planning was meticulous. The landing beaches were flanked by French batteries, and the frontage would have to be small enough to avoid the fire from French guns. There could be no fire support from the fleet, as the shallow, sloping seabed would hold the fleet some five miles offshore.

Abercromby stationed marker boats to keep the landing boats from straying into range of the French guns. The landing force was arranged into linear assault waves, with guide boats to keep the waves organized. The first wave carried infantry in flat-bottomed barges, each loaded with 50 troops. The plan assured that the troops would come ashore as coherent units, not the usual practice of dumping troops higgledy-piggledy. The grenadier companies stationed on the right flank of each regiment carried the regimental colors as a marking point to help regiments assemble. A second wave was carried in ships' boats, and transferred to the returning barges. A third wave consisted of towed boats carrying the artillery. In another deviation from the usual British practice of winging it, the entire plan was rehearsed at Marmorice Bay on the Turkish coast.

The only glitch came when for some reason on March 1 Admiral Keith paraded the fleet within sight of the French position at Alexandria. The landings were delayed by a storm, but on the morning of March 7 the British attacked. Despite the support of shallow-draft gunboats, several landing barges were struck by French artillery. Once ashore troops were able to quickly form into organized units, and resisted French counterattacks. The attackers moved quickly inland, establishing a deep beachhead.

On March 21 Abercromby was wounded, and died a week later. Along with the imaginative Abercromby died the immediate future of modern amphibious assault. Many of his ideas would not be seen again for 120 years.

ASSESSMENT: An outstanding success, lessons and innovations of which were ignored by a hidebound military and naval bureaucracy.

The overseas war between Napoleon and England was primarily for the control of the Caribbean, with major land campaigns on Santo Domingo. In 1804 an unopposed British expedition captured Diamond Rock, a tiny cliff-bound island, and emplaced cannons that dominated the approaches to Fort-de-France on Martinique. A nocturnal French counter-landing was aborted when the boats were swept out to sea by strong currents. A second attempt on May 31, 1805 succeeded in landing on a tiny beach, but without ladders the French could not scale the cliffs. The small garrison was finally forced to surrender from lack of water. The later British invasion of the Danish West Indies was bloodless. The British eventually began to systematically eliminate the isolated French colonies that served as bases for privateers.

The War of 1812

The peripheral war between the United States and Britain saw a number of amphibious and riverine campaigns, largely because land communications remained so poor. The British for most of the war contented themselves with operations against the fledgling American Navy, and blockading the American east coast ports. As a result much of the early part of the war consisted of fighting along the Canadian border.

On April 27, 1813 an American force landed on the Canadian shore of Lake Ontario, undefended save for some snipers. The Americans quickly assembled, attacked from the landward side, and captured York (modern Toronto). Their victory was for naught since the British retreated to the more defensible naval base at Kingston. The landing force was withdrawn after looting the town of stores, to prepare for an attack on Kingston.

Fort George, Canada, May 25–27, 1813

On May 25 the Americans began to bombard the town and naval base from vessels on the lake, and from Fort Niagara on the opposite shore. At dawn on May 27 the Americans staged a landing west of the fort, opposed by British troops and Canadian militia who charged into the water, but grapeshot from the American vessels drove off these counterattacks. The Americans advanced inland, were stalled by a resolute defense, but again effective gunfire support from the ships decided the issue. The British abandoned the fort without any real resistance.

On May 29 a retaliatory British expedition to destroy the American base where their ships were constructed, the second battle of Sacket's Harbor, was less effective as attacks were staunchly resisted by American regulars and militia. The Americans fell back into blockhouses and the British, unable to get artillery ashore, were forced to withdraw.

The Fort George attack was a success with minor casualties, largely because of careful planning by two future luminaries, army colonel Winfield Scott and navy master commandant Oliver Hazard Perry. The British and Canadians withdrew to the west, but the American army was slow to pursue the retreating enemy. After an ambush and defeat at Stoney Creek (June 6) the Americans retreated back toward Kingston, and the invasion of Canada stalled.

In the spring of 1814 the British launched another raid directed at lightly defended Fort Ontario that defended Oswego, New York. The landing force was small, as the governor-general of Canada declined to provide adequate forces. On May 6 Royal Marines, Canadian militia, and sailors attacked and captured the fort. British marines and sailors tried to intercept retreating Americans, but were ambushed with the loss of 200 men killed or captured.

In July 1812 the British had seized Mackinac Island that dominated the passage between lakes Huron and Michigan. On June 26, 1813 the Americans began to shell the main British defenses, and landed on August 4. The British commander sallied out to meet the Americans. In a hard fought battle the landing force was defeated and forced to withdraw.

The Chesapeake Bay Campaign,
August–September 1814

In 1813 the British had established a base on Tangier Island at the mouth of Chesapeake Bay to interrupt trade through the important port of Baltimore, from whence they staged raids on Virginia and Maryland. The largest of these raids resulted in the battle of Craney Island, June 22, 1813. A strong force of Royal Marines, army regulars, and militia landed on the mainland but were repulsed when they tried to cross a marsh onto the island. The British quickly staged a second landing on the east side of the island, only to be again driven off by artillery fire. The battle prevented British seizure of the strategic port of Norfolk, Virginia.

The defeat and exile of Napoleon freed up major British forces that began to be felt in the campaigns of late summer 1814. The American capital at Washington City was considered strategically inconsequential, but on August 19 the British landed and began to march on Washington City while ships moved up the bay. Over August 29–September 2 the British raided and briefly occupied Alexandria, Virginia. On August 24 the British inflicted a humiliating defeat on the Americans at Bladensburg, Maryland, and then marched onward to capture and burn Washington City.

The British next turned their attentions to Baltimore, where the Americans had constructed state-of-the-art Fort McHenry. On September 13 a British fleet commenced a 25-hour bombardment, and attempted a small amphibious assault near the fort. Unable to advance past the fort into the Patapsco River, and with their ammunition exhausted, the British sailed away, effectively ending the threat of further invasions along the east coast.

The successful defense of Baltimore was a huge coup for the Americans. The spectacular but unsuccessful bombardment of **Fort McHenry** was immortalized by Francis Scott Key in *The Star Spangled Banner*.

The Gulf Coast Campaign, September 1814–January 1815

The British turned their attention to the Gulf Coast of America. The United States had purchased the Louisiana territory from Napoleon in 1803. New Orleans, and to a lesser extent Mobile, were the transshipment points for goods moving in and out of the vast area west of the Appalachian Mountains.

The British recognized that control of New Orleans and Mobile would strangle American mid-continent trade, and result in British control of a vast swath of territory from Louisiana to eastern Canada. The British had equipped a rebellious faction in a Creek civil war that evolved into the Red Stick War of 1813–1814 against the United States. British agents operated with impunity through the Spanish West Florida ports of Mobile and Pensacola. Once the Red Sticks were defeated, American General Andrew Jackson was determined to eliminate British trade with the tribes. But with the defeat of Napoleon, huge numbers of veteran British troops were now available. The capture of New Orleans would be the culmination of the most ambitious and strategically significant British amphibious campaign ever conceived.

Jackson occupied Mobile in September 1814. On September 13 the British attacked crude Fort Bowyer on Dauphin Island that guarded the approaches to Mobile Bay, but were repulsed. The next town to fall to Jackson was Pensacola. The sea gave the British greater strategic mobility, but they squandered its potential. Marching overland, Jackson arrived in New Orleans in December, and set about preparing a defense with a motley assortment of Army regulars, and state and local militias, some of whom were unarmed. The city sits far up the winding Mississippi River, and approaching it was dependent upon fickle winds, complicated by two forts that dominated sharp bends.

Instead of the river approach, the British routed a flotilla of American gunboats on Lake Bourgne, actually a bay east of the city. Troops and heavy artillery were laboriously moved through the coastal swamps. Then the British encamped and dallied for weeks. On January 8, 1815 they launched a frontal assault against

The British initial landings to attack New Orleans in late 1814 were well executed despite great difficulties. The campaign failed when a second amphibious operation on the Mississippi River was unable to outflank the main American defenses. (National Archives)

Line Jackson, a ditch and crude mud wall at the narrowest point between the river and swamps to the north. A lesser-known but crucial part of the plan was a shore-to-shore attack up the opposite side of the river to capture lightly held American secondary defenses and enfilade Line Jackson with artillery. The landing failed because of unanticipated river currents, the frontal attack on the main American position stalled, and the British suffered the most lopsided defeat in their military history.

For nine days the British laboriously worked ships upriver to bombard the forts, without success. On January 19 they undertook a very difficult retreat and amphibious evacuation, unmolested by Jackson. The fleet and embarked army sailed away, to again attempt the capture of Mobile. The British landed miles from Fort Bowyer on February 8, and after a brief siege the fort surrendered on February 12. It was all in vain. A treaty had been signed on December 24, but the news did not reach Mobile until February 13.

ASSESSMENT: Given the enormous difficulties, the amphibious phase was as well executed as possible. A large army had been landed and its artillery moved through extraordinarily difficult terrain by brute manpower. The success was undone by the failure of the subsequent land campaign and secondary landing. The battle had immense geopolitical consequences, removing remaining British influence in southern North America, and assuring the westward expansion of the United States.

Through most of its early history the French Troupes de Marine and several similar organizations were charged with coastal defense. The early French experience was not particularly noted for amphibious operations, and many, like the 1830 invasion of Algiers, went unopposed.

As American global commerce grew, so did the potential for getting involved in overseas conflicts. On February 1831 Sumatran tribesmen attacked an American merchant ship that had come to pick up a cargo of pepper, killing three and plundering the cargo. The Dutch launched a punitive land campaign, but were limited by the potential for conflict with Britain. Newly elected President Andrew Jackson had no such qualms, and in 1832 an American amphibious raid burned Malay trading vessels in the port of Kuala Batu, captured four forts, and plundered the town. A second such incident prompted another incursion on January 1, 1839. A landing force burned the village of Muckle. The consequences of piracy were apparent, and no further incidents occurred.

Amphibious operations and fighting between white colonists and Native Americans are not typically associated with each other, but riverine operations played a significant role from the earliest days of European colonization, and continued through the Red Stick War. The Seminole War and Second Creek War (1836–1842) carried inland operations to a new level. The Seminole were an offshoot of the Creek Nation, absorbed diehards from the Red Stick War, and both fought a long and frustrating war against white settlers in the swamps and marshes of central Florida. With land transportation impossible, it was a war of canoes and small boats, ambushes, and tiny amphibious raids by American sailors, marines, and soldiers on hidden native villages. Ultimately the war just fizzled out without any treaty to end it; technically the Seminole Nation remains at war with the United States.

Vera Cruz (Mexican–American War), March 9, 1847

When war erupted over territorial disputes, it was obvious that no land invasion of Mexico was feasible. The only way to launch a decisive attack on the Mexican capital was by an invasion directed at the closest significant port, Vera Cruz. The problem was that the United States had never launched a large operation, much less one far from a base like those at Pensacola, Florida, 1,000 miles away.

Despite formidable technical and organizational problems, the landing force was loaded into ships' boats organized into landing waves. Gunboats drove off Mexican cavalry, and within five hours some 8,000 men were ashore. The US Army went on to stage a successful conventional siege of the port, and eventually attacked Mexico City.

The war saw the first use of steam-powered vessels in amphibious warfare. Steam vessels could move up rivers regardless of unpredictable winds. The Americans quickly seized the small Mexican port of Frontera, but the first attempt against two forts defending San Juan Bautista de Tabasco, 74 miles upriver, failed.

Captain Mathew Perry carefully organized and trained a naval brigade of sailors and marines, and transported them upriver in boats towed by four steam-powered warships. He landed with most of the troops some ten miles from the city, and marched overland to attack the fort at Accachappa. The main force then moved by land while a smaller detachment under Lieutenant David Dixon Porter worked past obstacles in the river. The two forces launched a combined land and amphibious assault on Fort Iturbide. The defenders fled. Porter and Dixon would go on to become major figures in the history of the US Navy.

ASSESSMENT: The war was the first successful major overseas operation by American forces. It demonstrated a capability for joint army–navy operations, provided early experience in naval gunfire support, and the innovative use of steam-powered vessels.

The Crimean War, 1853–1856

The next significant war broke out in 1853 with Russia and the Ottoman Empire squabbling over control of Jerusalem, and increasing unrest in the Ottoman-controlled Balkans. Britain and France aligned themselves with the Turks, although their aims were not altruistic; expansionist Russia posed a threat to British interests in India and the truculent Afghanistan buffer state. Fighting spread into the Baltic, and a Russian campaign in the Balkans was inconclusive. The primary campaign would be against Russian bases at Odessa and Sevastopol in the Black Sea.

The British had lost most of their hard-won expertise in expeditionary warfare. The assembly of a large army was described by one officer as a "shambles", and the transport of the army from England to the Black Sea was worse.

In late August 1854 a Franco-British fleet moved to invade the Russian Crimea, but although transports were numerous, they were so packed with troops—incredibly, up to 2,000 on some ships—that sailors could not manage the vessels. The Crimean coast had not been reconnoitered, and more days were lost as the unwieldy fleet sailed along the coast searching for a suitable beach. In a farcical exchange the Russian civil authorities at the small port of Eupatoria allowed some of the invading army to land, provided that the troops allowed themselves to be fumigated to control infectious diseases, according to Russian health regulations.

The main landings on September 14 were chaotic, with misplaced marker buoys. Ships' boats could not beach, and sailors carried soldiers ashore in their arms to avoid soaking their weapons and equipment. Units milled about in confusion, but by nightfall 20,000 infantrymen were ashore. The circus atmosphere was interrupted by heavy rain and wind, and the troops huddled together without tents or adequate clothing.

The storm abated the next afternoon, and after more confusion it was decided to land the cavalry by lowering the horses, fully loaded, to swim ashore. Some immediately drowned, others died of exhaustion, and many swam out to sea. When the army marched toward Sevastopol on September 19 they were unopposed, but without adequate water. By nightfall the British alone had lost 362 dead and over 1,600 incapacitated by heat exhaustion. Worse was yet to come in this mismanaged war.

ASSESSMENT: In an oft-repeated pattern, the British had forgotten virtually all the hard-won lessons of previous wars. In the Crimean campaign incompetence reigned from top to bottom: the overall commander, elderly Lord Raglan, habitually referred to his French allies as "the enemy" and the Turkish allies as "bandits."

In the Baltic British and French forces conducted amphibious raids on Finnish ports and villages, but could not subdue the forts defending Helsinki. Attacks on Kota and Archangel on the White Sea failed, as did a major campaign against Kamchatka on Russia's Pacific coast.

As the United States continued to engage in growing international commerce, it became increasingly entangled in international incidents. During the Second Opium War between Britain and China, on November 1856 a small American landing in Canton resulted in no fighting, but as the landing force withdrew it was fired upon by Chinese hotheads. On November 16 a landing force captured one Chinese fort at the mouth of the Pearl River, and used its guns to bombard and capture a second. After heavy fighting and disproportionate Chinese casualties (about 500 versus 29), the landing force withdrew.

Other conflicts such as the French-Spanish conquest of Cochinchina (Vietnam) were more permanent. On September 1, 1858 the French captured modern Danang, followed by Saigon (February 17, 1859). The war was protracted and bitter. The French decided to concentrate forces on less resistant Saigon; the most notable amphibious operation was the successful evacuation of Danang on March 22, 1860.

The American Civil War, 1861–1865

The Crimean War had been a portent of things to come, with the extensive use of explosive naval shells, rapid-firing weapons, and other innovations. But the American Civil War would be the first true industrial war. In this type of war the Union had an inestimable advantage, with a ridiculous lead in industrial capacity, a stronger seagoing tradition (particularly in the New England states), and a more extensive and interconnected rail network. Control of the sea and limited land transport nullified any advantage the Confederacy gained from interior lines of communication. The dominant Union navy could seize ports around the periphery of the Confederacy, and, combined with a naval blockade, could limit the activities of Confederate commerce raiders and strangle foreign trade on which the Confederacy depended. Union naval superiority led to the capture of strategic ports like New Orleans and Mobile, often without significant opposition.

The initial Union amphibious effort was the August 28/29, 1861 capture of batteries defending the Cape Hatteras inlets to block passage of Confederate blockade runners and maritime raiders. Naval gunfire was effective in neutralizing the Confederate batteries, but troops were loaded into boats far out to sea. The landings were slow, and in the late afternoon winds produced high surf that left only 318 assorted troops isolated onshore. Their salvation was the limited numbers and lack of ammunition on the part of the defenders.

Combined operations by naval and land forces would be most keenly felt in riverine operations. Union dominance of the major rivers and their tributaries provided for rapid movement of troops and supplies. On November 7, 1861 steam-powered riverboats transported Union troops under Ulysses Grant, and provided crucial fire support that helped repulse a Confederate counterattack in the battle of Belmont (Missouri). In his western campaigns Grant increasingly relied upon riverine operations, a fact that would be less obvious in the eastern campaigns, though the relentless Union use of this capability grew steadily.

Burnside's Roanoke Campaign, February 7–8, 1862

Both Union generals Ambrose Burnside and George McClellan claimed to have proposed the concept of a special amphibious division as early as September 1861. This division, equipped with organic, shallow-draft boats and transport barges, was intended to threaten the rear of Confederate forces in Virginia. Burnside was given the task of organizing the amphibious division, but was forced by competition with the navy to settle for a strange assortment of mismatched vessels, many unsuited to shallow-water navigation.

Burnside was obsessed with logistics and transport, to the exclusion of a coherent tactical doctrine or an operational plan. His plan was simple: land as large a force as possible, and then wing it for the ensuing land campaign. Incredibly, no training was provided in such skills as landing from a boat.

The first Union amphibious attack in the Roanoke campaign of February 1862, during the American Civil War, was an example of extraordinarily poor planning: dump the troops onto the beach with no clear objective except to make a near-suicidal charge against the defenses. Currier and Ives print. (National Archives)

Burnside's troops were temporarily landed on desolate Hatteras Island, North Carolina, simply to get them off overcrowded ships. After delays caused by reconnaissance that failed to ascertain that many of his boats could not get across the submerged bar at the entry to Pamlico Sound, Burnside finally moved his disorganized fleet into the Sound.

The salvation of the Union plan was Confederate unpreparedness. The approaches were covered by poorly sited batteries with sand walls, equipped with obsolescent artillery. The defensive maneuver element consisted of two understrength militia regiments armed with a hodge-podge of weapons; some had only knives. The total rebel strength was about 2,700 men—at any given time a quarter of them were laid low by disease—to face Burnside's 13,000.

The temporary commander of the defenses modified his orders at the last moment, and was irresolute. In the confusion, Burnside's troops landed without gunfire support from either the naval force or the army gunboats. The actual landing, however, was well executed, with steam launches towing strings of overloaded boats close inshore, and then casting them off with sufficient momentum to help them make the beach. Four thousand men and some light artillery were put ashore in about 20 minutes. The commander of the Confederate artillery, as limited as it was but which could have wreaked havoc on the landing force, lost his nerve and withdrew without firing a shot.

Burnside's planning had not extended past the initial assault. Boats returned with no clear-cut idea of how to load or land following waves; efforts to land supporting artillery were chaotic. The next day the landing force finally went in pursuit of the retreating Confederates. The only defensive position blocked the single road that led along the island, but it was easily outflanked.

ASSESSMENT: Lack of practice for Union troops regarding amphibious landings. The initial landing was marred by poor army–navy coordination, and having no clear plan as to what was to be done after the troops were ashore. The expedition did, however, provide useful experience in the complexities of a large amphibious operation.

Fort Fisher, December 1864–January 1865

By late 1864 the last significant remaining seaport for Confederate blockade runners was Wilmington, North Carolina, where Fort Fisher protected a narrow channel through the offshore islands. The first attempt to reduce the fort was to run an old ship loaded with 235 tons of gunpowder ashore near the fort. It was detonated on December 24, with no effect whatsoever. By poor coordination the transports carrying the assault troops arrived the next day, and any dubious shock value was lost. Two thousand troops landed several miles north of the fort. After sporadic fighting the defenders were baffled by a Union re-embarkation; the Union commander was fearful of Confederate reinforcements. It was, in Ulysses Grant's words, "a gross and culpable failure."

Grant's iron hand descended upon the new operational commanders, with explicit orders that a second landing force was to be withdrawn only under his direct orders. On January 13 some 8,000 troops came ashore at a carefully chosen site several miles from the fort. On the morning of January 15 a full-scale land assault began, and after a vicious day-long battle, the fort surrendered to overwhelming force and continuous bombardment.

ASSESSMENT: An interesting example of the hare-brained ideas that too often creep into military planning: that detonating a ship offshore could somehow destroy a fort on land. The second, and successful, assault was marked by Grant's typically meticulous planning.

In the period following its Civil War the United States became even more active in international trade, with resulting small conflicts around the globe. In the period 1866–1889 naval landing forces intervened 24 times, most significantly in Korea, Egypt, and Panama.

In early 1871 tensions arose between Korea and the United States over imprisonment of merchants and sailors, and the Americans launched a punitive attack on forts defending the Han River. The landing party struggled across mud flats and launched a successful attack on the Kwang Fort. Defeating Koreans armed with ancient muskets and small cannons, the landing party blew up the fort and withdrew: both sides claimed victory.

Less well known is the War of the Pacific, the bloodiest war in South American history. Between April 1879 and October 1883 it pitted Chile against a Bolivian–Peruvian alliance. The battle of Pisagua on November 2, 1879 was a Chilean landing that established a beachhead, allowing the Chileans to launch the primary land campaign of the war. After a short bombardment the Chilean landings were reasonably well executed. The Chileans had constructed *chalanas*, flat-bottomed boats suitable for beaching in shallow water, and were able to put 1,200 troops ashore in the initial assault wave. In fierce fighting the landing force seized high ground that dominated the landing beaches, allowing the Chileans to pour more and more forces ashore.

In June and July 1882 the British and French launched an amphibious attack on Alexandria, Egypt, in the Anglo-Egyptian War. On July 11/12 a two-day Franco-English naval bombardment heavily damaged the city. Forewarned by the British, an American landing party was first ashore, and the Americans and British Royal Marines cooperated in firefighting, preventing looting, and protecting foreign citizens.

In 1885 a secessionist movement in Panama (then part of Colombia) threatened American commercial interests, and the railway that provided the only link between the Caribbean and Pacific. It also provided the excuse for exercise of an increasingly aggressive American foreign policy. The Marine Corps cobbled together two battalions, and the navy chartered civilian ships for transport. In the interim, parts of Panama City were protected by sailors and marines from the ships first on the scene. The landing force secured the railway with minimal opposition, even constructing special railway cars armed with cannons and Gatling guns. With the success of Colombian nationalist forces assured, the Americans withdrew.

ASSESSMENT: The Panama operation revealed the weakness of the American marines in any protracted land operation; without an adequate supply system, the marines relied entirely upon the army for basic necessities like cooking pots and tents. The delay in assembling an expeditionary force by stripping ship detachments and shore stations was becoming increasingly undesirable, suggesting a more permanent force was needed.

The Spanish-American War of 1898 was primarily a conventional one, but witnessed an increasing role for the United States Marine Corps as expeditionary troops, and the formation of a large unit, Huntington's Battalion, for duty in Cuba. From the beginning the battalion encountered an old problem. The captain of the transport USS *Panther* wanted to dump the marines and have his ship assume a more high-profile role as a merchant cruiser. The battalion was put ashore in Key West.

A more visionary Rear Admiral William Sampson took charge and assigned the battalion to capture a much-needed coaling facility at Guantanamo Bay, Cuba. The landing was unopposed, and the marines established a shallow beachhead. A relatively minor Spanish counterattack disrupted the American camp and resulted in an attack by the marines that inflicted heavy casualties, and assured that there would be no further interference with naval operations.

As with the Whitehaven Raid, the actions of Huntington's Battalion would have effects disproportionate to its minor military significance. It was the first action reported "from the scene" by the news media, and provided considerable publicity for a lesser-known branch of the US military. More importantly, the war ushered in a new age of naval warfare truly dominated by steam-powered battleships that unlike sailing ships required refueling stations. The navy would in future rely heavily upon the capture and defense of advanced land bases to support operations, but the US Army was simply not interested in supporting the navy.

Who would fill the new role? The answer to that question would lead to a painful and protracted bureaucratic struggle that would revolutionize amphibious warfare.

Ignored by most of the world, a new power was also arising in Asia. Japan was striving to become a world power, and engaged in various offensives in Manchuria, Korea, mainland China, and Formosa. The First Sino-Japanese War (1894–1895) provided little in the way of amphibious experience, but set the stage for the rise of Imperial Japan as a regional power.

Japanese expansionism led to clashes with Czarist Russia, which had leased Port Arthur from China, since its own port at Vladivostok was not useable in winter. There was also considerable friction over who would control Manchuria and Korea. The Russo-Japanese War (1904–1905) was primarily a land and naval conflict, but Japan conducted a number of unopposed amphibious landings, most notably at Chemulpo Bay, west of Seoul. The minor landings in Korea, and particularly at Chemulpo Bay, had long-term significance in that they led the Imperial Army to realize the importance of amphibious warfare to an island nation.

CHAPTER 4

~~~~~~~~~~~~~~~~~~~~~~~~~~~~~~~~~~~~~~

THE AMERICAN ADVANCED BASE FORCE CONCEPT, AND THE GREAT WAR OF 1914–1918

*"A Marine should be sworn to the patient endurance of hardships,
like the ancient knights; and it is not the least of these necessary
hardships to have to serve with sailors."*

Field Marshal Bernard Montgomery

In 1900 the US Navy formed the General Board to assess the defense of its new empire against the threat posed by Germany's purchase of former Spanish possessions, especially the remainder of the Marianas, and the Caroline Islands. Navy and Army strategies had long been at odds, disagreement grew more acrimonious with the 1903 creation of the Army–Navy Joint Board, and boiled over in a dispute about how to defend the Philippines. Clearly the navy would have to somehow bear the responsibility of defending the approaches to the Panama Canal and the sea lanes to the Philippines without pre-existing bases.

Commandant Charles Heywood was both reluctant to give up the marines' traditional roles, and wary of inadequate funding. Exercises in 1903 and 1904 revealed old and new problems. In one exercise the captain of the transport USS *Panther* insisted that the marines perform routine ship board maintenance at the expense of their training. Efforts to practice construction of an advanced base at Subic Bay in the Philippines led an outraged (and influential) Major General Leonard Wood to complain that the Navy was usurping the army's role there.

Not even the possible outbreak of war with expansionist Japan in 1907 had much immediate effect, but the concept of an advanced base force slowly gained traction among more visionary Marine Corps officers. Still, neither the scheduling of joint Navy–Marine fleet exercises in 1913, nor another diplomatic clash with Japan, brought about much progress. A major culprit was money. The navy still preferred to put its money into battleships rather than colliers or troop transports. The crucial shift toward more emphasis on the expeditionary role would come in Mexico.

The first experience in what would be the birth of modern amphibious warfare was a sideshow to the Great War. In early 1914 Mexico was in the throes of civil war, and the moralistic American president, Woodrow Wilson, was seeking an excuse to confront the brutal dictator Victoriano Huerta. One of Huerta's local commanders detained some American sailors in Tampico, and the Americans learned of a major German shipment of arms to the Huerta regime.

For years the American Navy had been prodding the Marine Corps to develop its Advanced Base Force for the seizure and defense of advanced naval bases. The Navy and Marines had just completed a major amphibious rehearsal at Culebra Island, off the eastern tip of Puerto Rico, when Wilson elected to intervene in Mexico. The first major objective would be the port of Vera Cruz, Mexico's gateway to Mexico City and foremost oil export facility. The troops of the Advanced Base Force left behind their heavy equipment and sailed aboard the Navy's USS *Hancock* and the USS *Prairie*, converted ocean liners. Other ships like the collier USS *Jupiter* were pressed into service, and civilian ships were chartered. Manpower would come from the shipboard detachments of battleships of the Atlantic Fleet, and men combed out from shore duties.

On April 21 the local naval commander ordered a landing by a mixed force of sailors and marines, before the arrival of major Marine Corps forces. By the middle of the next day major Marine detachments were ashore, and the troops were fighting block-by-block through the city.

The US Army actually possessed a much larger organic transport capability, with four troop transports sitting in Galveston, and more

The coal transport USS *Jupiter* had a long and distinguished, though little-known, career. After serving as a troop transport it returned to its original mission. It was the first American ship converted to utilize experimental electric-turbine propulsion. Renamed the **USS Langley**, she underwent extensive conversion, and was recommissioned as the US Navy's first aircraft carrier in 1922. In 1936–1937 she was converted to a seaplane tender. *Langley* was scuttled after suffering irreparable damage in a Japanese aerial attack in 1942.

Veracruz, 1914. American troops loaded into ships' boats were towed close to shore by the steam launch at right, and left to run onto the beach under their own momentum. The technique had not changed since the Battle of Aboukir Bay in 1801. (Library of Congress)

chartered civilian ships. Nevertheless, the Army was slower off the mark, and did not arrive until April 29, long after hostilities had for all practical purposes ended.

Huerta went into exile, and no advance on Mexico City materialized. That was fortunate, since both the Army and Marine Corps were grossly unprepared for a land campaign.

ASSESSMENT: The Mexican adventure was a masterpiece of improvisation, and demonstrated that an expeditionary force actually could be quickly organized and successfully sent into action. Important lessons were learned about strategic transport; joint operations among Army, Navy, and Marine Corps forces; and urban warfare. The primary shortcoming identified was that the Marine Corps was ill-prepared for the logistical challenges of a land campaign. The US Army was better prepared for a land campaign, but slower to react. Even today the complementary nature of the two services remains apparent: the Marines are better suited to rapid deployment and quickly forcing entry into a hostile environment, with follow-on Army forces better suited to the long campaigns that follow.

African Misadventures, 1914

The Great War was primarily a land struggle in Europe, but amphibious operations to reduce Germany's African colonies led to the battle of Tanga (East Africa), November 3–5, 1914. The British commander gave the Germans a gentlemanly offer to surrender, which was declined. Troops were landed in the harbor and at beaches three miles east of the port. After a series of skirmishes the invaders captured the town, but the Germans rushed in reinforcements including *askaris* (native troops). Most of the landing force ran for the beach. Other units were attacked by swarms of angry bees, leading to the nickname "Battle of the Bees."

The victorious German force mistakenly withdrew, but the British force commander nevertheless ordered an ignominious evacuation. The British had suffered 847 casualties as opposed to 147 for the Germans, and the official British history of the war called it "one of the most notable failures in British military history." All in all, it was not an auspicious beginning.

Gallipoli, April 25, 1915–January 9, 1916

One amphibious operation—Gallipoli—eventually overshadowed all others for decades to come. The Gallipoli campaign was the brainchild of First Sea Lord Winston Churchill, and was intended to both open a southern line of communications with Russia through the Dardanelles, and knock Germany's eastern ally, the tottering Ottoman Empire, out of the war.

Considerable effort was invested in preparations, including the construction and towing to the Aegean Sea of 200 hastily designed landing boats called 'X' Lighters or Black Beetles. Based on Thames cargo barges, they each carried 500 men and were lightly armored. A narrow drop-ramp was provided at the front to disembark troops, but the rear of the ramp was high enough above the interior deck to make it unsuitable for anything but light artillery or mules. Some were modified as cargo barges and drinking-water tankers.

The Turks were aware of the Allied plans, particularly after a disastrous March 18 Allied attempt to force a passage through the straits by battleships that ran afoul of mines. A plan was hastily conceived to land on the Gallipoli peninsula, and sweep north to eliminate Turkish shore batteries that prevented minesweeping operations. The primary problem was that the Allies would have to fight their way along some 30 miles of rugged, and largely roadless terrain to reach the opening into the Sea of Marmara, the southwestern extension of the Black Sea. It was a foredoomed version of Burnside's 1862 campaign against Roanoke, but without the overwhelming numerical superiority and across far worse terrain. And it would leave the Turks still in possession of the eastern shore.

Given a month's respite, the Turks prepared shore batteries, trenches, and barbed-wire obstacles that extended down to the water's edge at potential landing sites. Hills overlooked many of the narrow beaches, and cliff-bounded promontories enfiladed landing sites. Once ashore the troops would have to move quickly up into the hills along narrow footpaths to establish a viable beachhead.

On the morning of April 25, 1915 cruisers and battleships of the combined British, French, and Russian fleets delivered an unobserved area bombardment directed at the crests of the hills that overlooked the landing beaches and in the valleys behind. A British officer noted that although the bombardment created much smoke and dust, it might have been better had small ships moved inshore that "could have searched out every cranny where a machine gun might be." But the captains of the smaller ships were unwilling to move within range of the shore batteries.

The Allied joint operation was cobbled together, no real improvements had been made in amphibious doctrine, and some lessons had been completely forgotten. The first assault waves were loaded into lifeboats and cutters, towed toward shore behind steam launches, but there were no wave guide boats or marker boats.

Another "innovation" that harkened back to the British privateer attack on Recife was a sacrificial landing ship. The old British collier *River Clyde* had hatchways cut into the sides of the hull, with gangways that could be dropped down the sides. The ship, carrying 2,000 troops, was driven aground at full speed on V Beach, near the tip of the peninsula. The men disembarked under heavy fire onto a floating bridge hastily erected by the ship's crew. A major accomplishment of the *Clyde* was to draw intense Turkish fire that might have been directed elsewhere, and the survivors were driven back to the dubious shelter of the ship until nightfall.

Heavy losses were suffered in trying to move inland. Units became disoriented in the rugged terrain, and the landing forces stalled on the beaches before nightfall. At the southern tip British forces were able to advance three miles and capture the strategic village of Krithia, but without any clear orders to exploit this coup, withdrew to the beach. Some officers misinterpreted orders and forbade their men to dig in under heavy fire. Only the Australians at "Anzac Cove" north of Kaba Tepe near the northern flank gained the controlling heights behind the beach.

The next morning the true extent of the confusion was apparent. One regiment had been virtually annihilated, and on some beaches the landing force had been driven back into the sea. The struggle to expand the beachheads was already bogging down. Eventually the Allies were able to put ashore a force of some 490,000 troops, but remained penned into the shallow beachheads by 315,000 Turkish troops.

The innovative X Lighters did not make an appearance until secondary landings at Suvla Bay on August 6. After suffering nearly 302,000 casualties the beachheads were evacuated in the first week of January 1916, with the loss of much artillery, vehicles, and valuable mules.

ASSESSMENT: Ill-conceived from the beginning, the operation was destined to failure both tactically and strategically. The invasion force was cobbled together, with unsuitable equipment, but even so these were not the primary causes of failure. The immediate tactical failure was inability, in some cases unwillingness, to quickly push the Turks off of commanding terrain and establish a viable beachhead. Throughout the campaign Turkish artillery was able to bombard beaches at will. Other problems were unclear tactical goals, lack of maps and poor intelligence, inadequately trained troops, insufficient artillery, and overconfidence in the face of unexpected Turkish resolve supplemented by German advisors. Even had the Allies been able to establish a viable beachhead, they faced even larger problems, primarily a long slog across easily defensible mountainous terrain in a narrow peninsula. The ostensible goal was to eliminate Turkish batteries, but the campaign would have left the easily reinforced eastern shore in Ottoman hands. Almost all these failures were lost in subsequent efforts to affix or avoid blame. The consensus that emerged was that machine guns and artillery had rendered amphibious assaults impossible, resulting in a willful 25-year abandonment of amphibious doctrine by most armies. In the longer term, Gallipoli's greatest contribution was that it provided useful lessons of what *not* to do in an amphibious campaign.

For most of the war the eastern Baltic was relatively quiet, but by late 1917 Russia was in the throes of the Bolshevik Revolution. The German perceived a chance to capture Petrograd (St. Petersburg) by invading the semi-autonomous Russian "governate" of Estonia. Two early landing operations using civilian fishing trawlers and other vessels failed, but on October 12/13 the Germans secured a lodgment on Hiiumana Island. The Russian fleet was forced to withdraw from the region, but despite inflicting heavy Russian casualties, the campaign ended on October 20, with no material effect on the war.

British Coastal Raids, April–May 1918

During the course of the war Germany had shifted significant numbers of submarines to the Belgian ports of Ostend and Zeebrugge. Their operations in the North Sea and English Channel disrupted transport between France and England, and land offensives (including the Ypres battle) were unsuccessful in ousting the Germans. Bombardment by British long-range artillery partially disrupted operations from Ostend, but naval bombardment of Zeebrugge was ineffective. It was decided to sink blockships to close the Zeebrugge harbor, located several miles inland up a narrow channel.

On the night of April 22/23 the British struck at the two ports using specially modified ships and a Royal Marine battalion. At Zeebrugge the obsolete cruiser HMS *Vindictive*, modified to carry troops and deploy gangways to disgorge them, jammed itself against the seaward side of the Mole—a large stone breakwater and artificial island enclosing the harbor—just after midnight. Two smaller river ferries pushed *Vindictive* against the Mole, and troops were landed from all three. A submarine packed with explosives was detonated to demolish a viaduct that connected the Mole to the mainland, preventing German reinforcement. The Royal Marine storming parties did not succeed in taking the German battery at the end of the Mole, but did distract the gunners from firing upon three blockships as they passed. One ran aground, but two others reached the canal connecting to the inland port, and detonated explosives that blew their bottoms out. By 0100 hours the troops were back aboard ship, and the last, *Vindictive*, drew out of range of German guns.

A simultaneous attack on Ostend was an abject failure as German *Seebataillons* (marines) drove off the attackers. On May 9 the British tried again at Ostend, assisted by long-range land artillery fire and air attacks. Attacking through a dense fog, the British became disoriented and sank *Vindictive* in a position that only partially blocked the channel. Only one of the small boats intended to evacuate *Vindictive*'s crew made it into the harbor, though it returned several times to search for survivors.

ASSESSMENT: Though probably as well-executed as was possible under the circumstances, the raids only partially closed the two ports. Large warships were trapped, but smaller craft and submarines could pass the wrecks, particularly at high tide. The raids failed to achieve their primary objectives.

Other proposed amphibious operations never came to pass, including a fanciful British scheme to land heavy tanks from large barges to outflank German forces in the Passchendaele (Third Ypres) Offensive of 1917. The Russians constructed two types of landing craft based on commercial cargo carriers for use in a canceled scheme for landings in the Sea of Marmara.

CHAPTER 5

THE INTERWAR PERIOD AND DEVELOPMENT OF A MODERN DOCTRINE

> *"[T]he enemy would hold his main fleet within his defense line; fleet units must be husbanded; preliminary activities of the U.S fleet must be accomplished with a minimum of assets; Marine Corps forces must be self-sustaining; long, drawn-out operations must be avoided to afford the greatest protection to the fleet; sea objectives must include a fleet anchorage."*

Operation Plan 712J—Advanced Base Operations in Micronesia, 23 July 1921

The Great War profoundly altered the global balance of power. The European powers were debilitated by the cost. Japan was industrializing at a breakneck pace, but with a homeland poor in resources. Some could be obtained by the conquest of mainland China, Korea, and Manchuria, and most others could be obtained from Southeast Asia and the East Indies. Japanese militarists came to see the conquest of these regions as Japan's destiny, but to conquer and control these regions Japan would need to project military and naval power.

After the Gallipoli disaster the military experts of European nations concluded that the amphibious campaign belonged to the past. Generals thought that deep-water harbors were indispensable to land troops that would engage in massive land battles. This required the ports and surrounding land and waters to be in friendly hands, so colonial powers concentrated on major fortification programs at places like Singapore and Hong Kong.

The British continued to experiment with landing craft, with squabbling between the Army and Royal Navy as to who should pay the bill. The result was the Motor Landing Craft, a boxy vessel capable of landing a light tank from a bow ramp, and incorporating an early type of water-jet propulsion. Despite its promise, by 1940 the Royal Navy possessed only nine.

The problem remained how to transport and launch landing craft that had no independent seagoing capability. Sir Roland Baker designed a number of vessels for the purpose; the first was the 1940 Landing Ship Stern Chute, a modified train ferry that launched preloaded landing craft off a stern ramp. HMS *Daffodil* and *Iris* were still not long-range transports, so his next effort was the Landing Ship Gantry, a modified oil tanker that deposited loaded landing craft into the water with two huge cranes. Lifting capacity was limited to the boat plus ten tons of cargo, useless for landing tanks. Three belatedly entered service in early 1941.

A far worse problem was that inter-service squabbling slowed the development of any cohesive British amphibious doctrine.

Japan foresaw the need for amphibious operations, but the development of suitable equipment, and in particular doctrine, was impeded by an inter-service rivalry worse than in any other nation. The Imperial Army and Navy competed not only for funding and resources, but increasingly for political power. The Imperial Army forged ahead on the development of an amphibious capability as the Navy concentrated on confronting the American and British fleets.

As early as 1918 Japan began to establish a very simple amphibious doctrine, teach courses, write manuals, and rehearse amphibious operations. A specialized landing boat needed to be designed to bring troops and heavy equipment ashore, and, in 1925, the *Daihatsu* was born. The Daihatsu profoundly influenced the evolution of landing craft. The original Daihatsu was a 56-foot self-propelled wooden barge with a front ramp, capable of carrying a light tank (7.4 tons) or 70 men. An improved version, the 1940 Toku Daihatsu, was of steel construction and could carry a 16-ton tank; only about 160 were built.

The Japanese *rikusentai* (Special Naval Landing Force, or naval infantry) and Special Base Forces were equipped with heavy

Observation of landing craft like this Japanese Daihatsu landing barge, captured and used by the US Army in the Aleutians, greatly influenced the design of the larger and more versatile American designs. (Library of Congress)

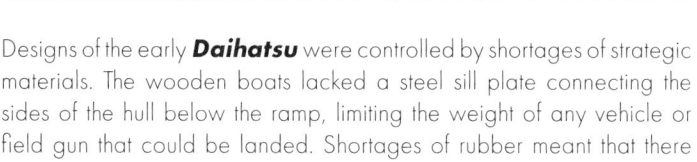

Designs of the early **Daihatsu** were controlled by shortages of strategic materials. The wooden boats lacked a steel sill plate connecting the sides of the hull below the ramp, limiting the weight of any vehicle or field gun that could be landed. Shortages of rubber meant that there was no adequate gasket around the ramp, and the ramp opening had to be kept as high above water as possible. The result was that any vehicle or artillery piece had to be moved up a steep internal ramp, and then down an even steeper ramp onto the beach.

equipment like tanks and artillery, but many assaults during the early war years would be made using ships' boats or *shohatsu*, 35-foot simple barges with a conventional hull and an open well-deck.

In the 1932 expansion into China most operations were successful due more to the lack of ability in the Chinese Army, and because Japanese mostly selected unopposed landing sites. The Imperial Army and Navy briefly worked to improve amphibious

Isakov's doctrine classified landings into three categories: strategic, tactical and raiding. A *strategic landing* was designed to open a new front, and involved large units from division to army corps scale. The battalion- to division-size *tactical landing* was intended to relieve pressure on ground troops deployed in a land battle. A smaller *raid* caused confusion among the enemy and served as a diversion for larger landings or land operations.

doctrine, but in the late 1930s the army–navy political animosity again grew, and amphibious operations nearly disappeared from manuals and courses. The rift was never fully healed, so the Japanese never developed a truly coherent amphibious doctrine. Amphibious operations were marred by poor communications, uncoordinated air and naval gunfire support, and poor logistics, among numerous other issues.

The Soviets foresaw the need for amphibious operations on the bordering seas. They began work on an amphibious doctrine under the guidance of Admiral Ivan Stepanovitch Isakov. By 1930 he became the chief of staff of the Baltic Sea Fleet, and among other duties was in charge of establishing an amphibious doctrine.

According to Isakov, the success of an amphibious assault was determined by several factors: (1) the need for a coordinated plan, (2) knowledge of the weather and tides, (3) training and fleet coordination, (4) selection of a suitable landing site, and (5) secrecy regarding the nature of the objective.

American experts were divided. The US Army followed the European enthusiasm for mechanized warfare and combined arms tactics. A number of officers, including Major George Patton, were interested in amphibious warfare, but the Army as a whole had little institutional interest.

The US Navy, realized the necessity of an amphibious capability in anticipation of a future war against Japan. Soon after the end of World War I, the United States established plans for potential wars against other nations. In 1919 German colonial possessions in

Major Earl H. "Pete" Ellis's prophetic 1921 "Advanced Base Operations in Micronesia" laid the basis for amphibious assault techniques used by all Allied forces in World War II, and even predicted in detail the strategy of the war in the Pacific. (Marine Corps History Division)

the Pacific, including the Caroline, Marshall and Marianas islands (except Guam), were mandated to Japan. Japan could now threaten the communication lines between America, its Pacific colonies of Guam and the Philippine Islands, and allies like Australia.

"War Plan Orange" foresaw a war in which Japan was to be defeated in a decisive naval battle near the Japanese Home Islands. The Navy recognized that it would have to capture advanced naval bases from Japan, but the Army was not interested in serving the needs of the Navy in the Pacific. The eventual solution came from a brilliant but eccentric Marine Corps officer, Major Earl H. "Pete" Ellis.

For two years, Ellis and a small staff worked on a masterpiece which described with prophetic precision the course of a Pacific war still two decades away. "Advanced Base Operations in Micronesia" was officially approved in July 1921 as Operation Plan 712H, the first truly comprehensive amphibious doctrine.

Ellis recommended that American-held islands be fortified and modernized as naval and/or air bases. A necessary mission would be the capture of additional islands. He recommended a campaign to capture the Marshall Islands and then the Caroline Islands in the Central Pacific. He suggested that the existing Advanced Base Force needed to be more specifically trained for amphibious assault.

In the attack phase, islands or group of islands would fall into two categories: "special objectives" which were expected to be centers of enemy resistance, and "occupation objectives" where little or no resistance was expected. He suggested multiple landing sites to disperse enemy resistance. The choice would be established by ground or air reconnaissance, and influenced by where troop transports could anchor away from enemy shore batteries. Ellis emphasized that the greatest elements of success were surprise and rapid maneuver to secure a viable beachhead. No delay should fall between each phase of the invasion, and each entity (beach parties, assault infantry, boats crew, guides, et cetera) should be perfectly coordinated so as not to give the enemy time to react.

Ellis predicted that the success depended upon who controlled the skies above the objective. The assault would be protected and supported by naval aircraft and naval gunfire support. Specially trained engineers would allow troops to quickly leave the shore. A communications plan should be instituted as early as possible for communicating between vessels offshore, assault troops, reconnaissance, naval and air support, et cetera. Likewise, logistics needed to be organized to bring sufficient troops and matériel ashore in a coordinated effort.

In 1923 Commandant John LeJeune approved Ellis's plan. By the end of the 1920s the War and Navy departments agreed to this new mission as perfectly fitting to the Marines because "of their constant association with Navy units." For this, they "will be given special preparation in the conduct of landing operations."

But this was theory. Many Marine Corps officers thought the Corps should fulfill army-like tasks and until 1926 Marine Corps Schools did not teach the amphibious role. The Navy did not devote sufficient attention to amphibious operations since it was busy with its own expansion. What most handicapped the establishment of a new doctrine was the lack of money, colonial deployments, and fighting in China and Nicaragua.

The small, newly created Expeditionary Force began its training. The first landing exercise took place in 1921 in the Caribbean and involved infantry, artillery, engineers, signals, chemical warfare, and aviation troops. As could be expected, the result was unsatisfactory. But persistence was the key word, and rehearsals continued. The seemingly simple task of disembarking troops from transports to

Landing armored vehicles proved to be a major problem in amphibious warfare. This King armored car will be unloaded with the aid of a wooden ramp constructed on the beach by engineers, hardly a viable technique in an assault landing. (Marine Corps History Division)

landing boats (ship's lifeboats) took months to master. Delays also applied to assault-wave coordination, and communication between units.

Several innovations were introduced during the 1924 Culebra exercise, among them a three-tank platoon of M1917 tanks. The tanks were unloaded at a pier and were utilized in a defensive role. John Walter Christie, an engineer and designer of military vehicles, had constructed an amphibious tank, a small-caliber cannon in an open-topped box, mounted on a wheel-track suspension. The vehicle was first lifted from a battleship onto a wooden frame fixed to the deck of a submarine that transported it close to shore where the submarine submerged, allowing the tank to float free. The vehicle crew refused to maneuver the little tank through the surf to the beach and development was abandoned.

Experimental landing craft were tested, without significant success. Nevertheless, one design was to become famous in the near future. One was a 50-foot landing boat equipped with a bow ramp that could disembark lightweight wheeled equipment. The idea of the bow ramp would later be reused by Andrew Higgins for his famous LCVP.

An early solution to landing vehicles included the awkward "beetle boats" designed by the US Navy Bureau of Ships, shown here in a 1920s landing rehearsal at Culebra. (Marine Corps History Division)

Exercises were disappointing because Ellis's work remained just a guideline to the establishment of a doctrine, and the exercises were not true tests of potential capabilities. During the 1924 rehearsal the attack force was outnumbered by the defenders, when it should have been the reverse. There were not enough boats to disembark troops. Naval bombardment was inefficient against the defenders' fixed positions. Medical supply was disembarked nine days after the landing because it was preloaded at the bottom of the holds. "In short," historians Jeter Isely and Philip Crowl concluded, "almost all the mistakes conceivable in a landing operation were made." This was perceived by some as discouraging, but the purpose of the training was to shed light on problems.

A number of lesser-known but significant exercises included a small 1925 "notional" invasion of Oahu by elements of the 4th Marines (Regiment). This exercise was notable in that it was observed by army officers, including the ambitious and hyperactive George Patton. Along with many other army officers, he would maintain an interest in amphibious doctrine.

1933 marked a turning point in the will of the Marine Corps to adopt an amphibious doctrine. The last troops left Nicaragua, and the Corps could now dedicate a large force to amphibious training.

Assistant Commandant of the Marine Corps, Major General John Russell Jr., suggested the creation of a force to be included in the fleet, under the fleet commander's orders. The Fleet Marine Force was born. Although weak (one infantry regiment, two batteries of 75mm pack howitzers, one battery of 50-caliber machine guns, and two aircraft groups), this force was to grow. Instructors now taught amphibious courses at the Marine Corps schools.

In 1934 the Navy and the Marine Corps *Tentative Manual for Landing Operations* was adopted. This manual was developed in a very innovative manner: a prolonged brainstorming session among officers in the new Fleet Marine Force. Each was asked to write down a list of things to be done from the beginning to the end of a landing. It was an exercise based on both intuition and common sense. The lists were studied by a smaller committee of nine officers who picked the ones that seemed the most interesting. The doctrine was born. From this work, the essential components of a landing operation were: (a) command relationships, (b) naval gunfire, (c) aerial support, (d) ship-to-shore movement, (e) securing a beachhead and (f) logistics.

From that point there were three improvements in the Marine Corps and Navy approach to the doctrine. Historical and theoretical studies of landing operations were increased in schools, cadets participated in annual landing exercises, and a program of technological development was organized.

The first annual landing exercise, Fleet Landing Exercise Number 1 (FLEX-1), was held in early 1935 in conjunction with elements of the fleet under the eyes of Army observers. The 5th Marine Regiment, less one battalion, formed the main body to which an artillery regiment and a Marine aerial observation squadron were attached. Though not realistic, it proved useful in the determination of which naval shells were capable of eliminating land targets.

The 1936 exercise saw the first use of cargo nets for disembarkation; previously infantry were unloaded from ship to landing craft using gangways. Spotters for naval artillery were put into planes to coordinate gunfire support.

The Navy was now beginning to accept the need for specialized amphibious assault ships. One measure was to convert obsolete

World War I "four-stacker" destroyers into small transports capable of launching landing boats. These Auxiliary, Personnel, Destroyers (APDs) were "high-speed transports" in name only, since half the ship's boilers and engines were removed to make space for troops. Exercises tested landings through mangrove swamps and reefs. The former went well while the tests showed that motor launches couldn't ground on reefs.

The US Army was belatedly showing an interest in amphibious warfare. The 1937 exercise was a joint Marine Corps–Army rehearsal, and led to more critical remarks. It proved that ordinary ships' boats were completely unsuitable, and it was confirmed that not all naval shells were suitable for gunfire support. Night landings were the subject of much criticism because they were risky for both the boats and the men: boats got lost in the dark, and terrain features were invisible, which made it problematic for units to locate themselves. The only way to make a successful night landing was to have the troopships closely approach the beach, a dangerous maneuver.

It was obvious that naval gunfire or planes could not destroy all enemy positions. Brigadier General James J. Meade suggested that more effort be devoted to accurately locate targets. In case air and naval gunfire support could not reach these targets, it was necessary that tanks accompany ground troops. Amphibious assault of a defended beach was analogous to trench warfare in World War I, where only tanks were able to break wire entanglements and silence the adversary's machine guns. Meade suggested that an increased number of tanks be employed during a landing, but boats large enough did not yet exist.

The effort to provide armored support led the Marines into one of its major dead ends, the development of a lightly armored "expeditionary tank." The primary development was the Marmon-Herrington Company series of "tankettes" of a type then popular in European armies. These vehicles were light, thinly armored, usually turretless, and armed only with machine guns. The problem remained that the vehicles had to be lifted with light ships' cranes and deposited onto a boat bobbing in the waves, so the weight was limited by the capabilities of existing cranes. Attempts were made

Without suitable tank landing craft, tanks had to be lifted into ordinary ships' boats with cranes, limiting weight and size. This Marmon-Herrington CTL-3A "tankette" is in use by the US Marines in August, 1941. (National Archives)

to equip traditional ship's boats with ramps, but the results were mediocre.

The solution came the next year, in 1938, with the first use of a specially designed navy tank lighter with a bow ramp that could safely land a tankette. Another significant improvement appeared when the 1939 exercise saw the testing of manufacturer Andrew J. Higgins new wooden landing craft. Designed to support oil drilling in the Mississippi Delta, it was of shallow draft and could beach and retract easily. At the suggestion of Marine Corps observers, Higgins modified his designs to include a bow door for easier unloading to produce the LCP(R). The Marines gave up on tankettes in favor of army tanks; Navy designs for a tank lighter were proving unsatisfactory. Higgins quickly built the prototype of a boat capable of carrying an army light tank. During a test a Navy-designed tank lighter nearly foundered, and had to be rescued by Higgins's boat. The Navy designs were quietly dropped in favor of the prototype for the Landing Craft, Mechanized or LCM-1.

Development of amphibious equipment had now reached a frenetic pace. Retired manufacturer Donald Roebling was working on a project to create a floating vehicle with tracks to rescue victims of hurricanes. The Marines immediately recognized its potential,

The various models of the Marmon-Herrington "tankettes" in the row at right marked successive attempts to develop a light armored vehicle that could be carried in small landing boats. Development of the LCM-1 allowed landing cannon-armed light tanks like those in the left row, rendering tankettes obsolete. (US Marine Corps via Ken Estes)

and in 1940 the first Landing Vehicle Tracked (LVT) was tested as a logistical vehicle. In this same year the Corps pressed the Navy to contract with Roebling to produce an armored variant equipped with a light tank turret.

In 1939 a long-anticipated conflict erupted when the Germano-Russian *blitzkrieg* overran Poland. Poland fell quickly, and German armies were reoriented westward. By the autumn of 1940 Denmark, France, Belgium and the Netherlands capitulated. With them, any hope for the Americans to land troops in a friendly port vanished.

Blindsided by this unexpected event, the US Army suddenly showed increased interest in landing operations and published *Field Manual 31-5*, a copy of the 1938 Navy *Fleet Training Publication 167*. In 1941 the Japanese attack on Pearl Harbor forced American entrance into the war, which led to a huge increase in the number

Andrew Higgins developed the LCM-1, capable of carrying and landing a light tank, at his own expense. In its first test the Higgins boat came to the rescue of a Navy-designed boat that was foundering in a storm. (National Archives)

The original LVT-1 "amtrac" was developed as a logistics vehicle. The US Marines pressed them into service as assault personnel carriers at Tarawa, and improved models became a mainstay of amphibious assaults. (Marine Corps Grey Research Center)

By 1939 the US Army was conducting a few full-scale **amphibious rehearsals**, but was hamstrung by the more important complexities of building a large national army. The Army suffered from the same stingy Congressional funding for development of new equipment that bedeviled the Marines. With troop training conducted using brooms as rifles, and trucks with canvas tarps labeled "TANK" on the sides, there were not that many funds for development of specialized equipment.

The Landing Ship, Tank (LST) was a major World War II British innovation that allowed depositing heavy vehicles directly onto the beach. There were never enough of these important vessels. The bulldozers of the Army Engineers, Navy Seabees, and Marine Corps Shore Parties were used to clear obstacles, or in this case to construct ramps for easier unloading on a Korean beach. (National Archives)

of Marine Corps, Army and Navy troops trained in amphibious warfare.

The fertile mind of Sir Roland Baker continued to stir, and the result was two of the iconic seagoing landing ships of all time. The Landing Ship Tank (LST) was a large flat-bottomed seagoing vessel with bow doors that could deposit tanks and heavy vehicles directly onto the beach. The Landing Ship Dock was a large transport

The British-designed Landing Ship Dock could carry pre-loaded landing craft or amphibious tractors internally, and release them through a large hatch at the rear. The USS Tortuga is shown releasing LVT(A)-4s in Korea, 1952. (Marine Corps History Division)

that could carry Higgins's new LCMs internally. Upon arrival at the objective the ship could ballast down, open a stern ramp, and launch LCMs preloaded with tanks or other vehicles. But in early 1942 production of adequate numbers of these vessels lay far in the future.

CHAPTER 6

~~~~~~~~~~~~~~~~~~~~~~~~~~~~~~~~~~~~~

AXIS DOMINATION

"The fruits of victory are tumbling into our mouths too quickly."

Emperor Hirohito, April 1942

The Axis nations were ill-prepared for war. Resources were limited and despite Japan's adventurism in Korea and China, practical expertise in large-scale amphibious operations was non-existent. Germany had no expertise at all—and no plans to develop any. Italy's colonial adventurism had demonstrated no need. The early Axis offensives were slapdash efforts.

Operation Weserubung, Norway, 1940

Lost in the history of World War II is the fact that the opening move on the Western Front was a German amphibious campaign. Norway attempted to remain neutral, but the Great Powers decided differently. German industry relied heavily upon high-grade Swedish iron ore that could only move through the ice-free harbor of Narvik, in northern Norway, and control of Norway would also assure that German surface ships could pass from the Baltic into the North Sea. The British wanted possession of Norwegian ports not only to disrupt the German iron ore supply, but to prevent their use as submarine bases. The problem was that neither side was prepared for an amphibious campaign. The advantage that the Germans possessed was that southern Norway was within range of fighter aircraft.

The Germans prepositioned merchant ships (most disguised as ships from neutral countries) loaded with supplies and ammunition in Norwegian ports. Troops would be brought in aboard warships in a last-minute dash from Germany. On April 9 the Germans launched a series of ground, airborne and seaborne attacks on Denmark and several harbors along the Norwegian coast. Without landing craft, the Germans relied heavily upon airborne landings. German troops successfully landed in the harbors of Kristiansand, Bergen, Trondheim, and Narvik.

At Oslo, the capital, coastal gunfire sank a German cruiser and prevented the Kriegsmarine from approaching the harbor. The city finally collapsed after 3,000 paratroopers were brought in. The static supply ships off the beachheads were vulnerable. At Narvik, the Royal Navy counterattacked and sank several ships and destroyers. The Germans learned a harsh lesson when the transport *Antaris H*, carrying 18 light tanks, was sunk by a Polish submarine. This forced the Germans to rush in three obsolescent heavy tanks built for propaganda purposes.

On April 18 British and French troops landed unopposed at Namsos and Andalsnes, but the Germans were determined to force them back, supported by superior aviation. At Narvik the Germans were thwarted by Norwegian resistance; the Germans held the port but were unable to make further progress. British, Polish and French troops were landed to try and reduce the Narvik pocket. French Foreign Legion troops were the first to undertake an opposed landing operation during World War II, supported by three French H-39 light tanks brought in aboard two British Motor Landing Craft and an LCM-1.

Despite fierce German resistance, the larger number of the attackers overwhelmed the defenders, but by May most of Norway was clearly in German hands, and the changing situation in France and Belgium forced an Allied evacuation.

ASSESSMENT: Despite the improvisations, for the Germans Norway had been a success and was the first air–sea combined operation of World War II. The method would eventually be repeated in Crete about a year later. The indirect attack undertaken by the Allies was a failure since the Germans were able to counter their effort with superior airpower. While the landings were unopposed, the French Foreign Legion proved it was necessary for attackers to outnumber the defenders to have any chance to break through a defended beach. The ultimate Allied downfall was the lack of air support.

Dunkirk, May 27–June 4, 1940

In mid-1940, the German *blitzkrieg* surprised the world. The attacking Germans, flooding through Belgium, were heading for Paris. All French efforts to stem the rout failed. The surrender of the Belgians opened a huge gap and large French and British forces were trapped in northern France. To prevent their best troops from falling into German hands, Winston Churchill ordered the evacuation of the British Expeditionary Force.

French and British troops fell back to several ports, but Dunkirk was chosen as the primary evacuation point because it was the least damaged by bombing, the broad beaches could in theory be used to assemble troops, and a belt of marshes and canals landward of the town would aid in defense.

Then Hitler made a controversial decision. The Germans would not exert full pressure against the trapped armies. The German Army was depleted by its rapid advances and an attack against the defenses promised heavy casualties. Over the objections of his generals, Hitler decided that the Luftwaffe would destroy the trapped armies.

A motley flotilla of ships and boats was hurriedly assembled to rescue the trapped soldiers. While two French divisions kept the Germans as far as possible from the port, troops were crowding into the harbor to embark on a cruiser and eight destroyers. The problem was that the ships could not load quickly enough in the congested harbor. When a call was issued for smaller civilian boats, numerous vessels with their volunteer civilian crews allowed the British to evacuate more soldiers from the open beaches. Despite German shelling and bombing, the British were able to evacuate 338,226 Allied troops—British for the most part. The remaining 35,000 troops surrendered to the Germans.

Churchill would rightly describe this rescue as a "miracle" which allowed the British to reorganize for the defense of Britain. But beyond the fact that thousands of troops were successfully evacuated, critical equipment and material was left behind. An armistice was signed with the French government on June 22, forcing the French expeditionary force to finally leave Norway.

ASSESSMENT: Probably the greatest and most strategically significant evacuation of an army in history, Operation *Dynamo* rescued the core of Britain's professional army. While it did not in actuality help preserve Britain from invasion, lost matériel could be replaced more quickly than trained soldiers.

The British Channel Islands, June–July 1940

Following the French capitulation of June 1940, German troops in the Cotentin peninsula could see, 20 miles to the west, the British islands of Guernsey and Jersey. The Germans expected resistance and considered an amphibious assault to take the islands. However the British decided not to waste resources to defend the islands. The islands surrendered to a German pilot who was forced to make an emergency landing.

Operation *Sea Lion*, 1940

As early as November 1939, the Germans considered the invasion of Great Britain one of the key points necessary for victory over the Allies, but several issues needed to be resolved even if the operation was about a year in the future. These included the availability of troop transports and landing craft. Now the Germans fell victim to their own success. The rapidity with which France collapsed was unexpected, and by mid-1940, the Kriegsmarine and Luftwaffe still had far to go to overcome their British counterparts. The Kriegsmarine had suffered irreplaceable losses during the Norway campaign; the only available ships were four cruisers and nine destroyers. It would fall to the Luftwaffe to annihilate the Royal Air Force and the ships defending the English Channel.

The Wehrmacht estimated that about 126,000 troops would be necessary to secure three landing sites. The general invasion plan set the pattern for most of the major operations by other nations for the remainder of the war. Nine infantry divisions would land near Portsmouth, Brighton and Dover, and two airborne divisions were to secure the areas inland. Artillery and armored units would land in the first hours of the invasion. Once ashore the armies would sweep north and around London to avoid becoming bogged down in slow and costly urban warfare.

In previous operations on the Continent, Germany had made some use of "fifth columns," local collaborationists who assisted military operations. In England there was no extensive collaborationist network. The Germans had used intelligence agents operating under the guise of tourists to compile extensive information on infrastructure—roads, railway lines, telephone and electrical systems, et cetera. These German preparations for operations after the invasion were thereby far more meticulous than the invasion plan itself.

One huge issue remained: how to carry major ground forces across the Channel? By August the Kriegsmarine succeeded in gathering about 2,000 small craft, mostly unsuitable civilian vessels like river ferryboats. Bulk cargo barges normally used to carry commodities like grain or coal were modified by cutting the bows off and fitting crude ramps. Many were damaged or sunk in harbors by concentrated RAF attacks.

The Germans recognized that **landing tanks** was necessary. In addition to modifying civilian bulk cargo barges by cutting off the bows and fitting crude ramps, about 400 light tanks were fitted with pontoons and propellers to cross short distances of shallow water. Another and far more hazardous solution was to waterproof light tanks, and equip them with large flexible air intake and exhaust tubes that connected to floats. The idea was to lower them into shallow water and have them drive across the sea bottom along a compass bearing.

By early September an armada of improvised landing craft was ready to cross the Channel, but the Luftwaffe had sustained so many losses that control of the air and sea surrounding the invasion site could not be guaranteed. Hitler decided to postpone the invasion to an unspecified date, and turned his interest to Russia for Operation *Barbarossa*. The titanic struggle between Nazi Germany and the Soviets would involve peripheral but significant amphibious operations.

Crete, May–June 1941

Britain had begun to develop Crete as a base for operations in the eastern Mediterranean, but German air attacks hindered transport of supplies and personnel to the isolated island. In late April Hitler approved Operation *Mercure*, a combined amphibious–airborne assault. The Germans had conducted successful airborne assaults in Europe, but an amphibious operation would be necessary to introduce heavy forces to counter 25 British tanks and British and Greek artillery.

The May 20 airborne landings went more or less according to plan, but the Axis forces had not established naval superiority. A May 22/23 attempt to land German reinforcements from a hastily assembled flotilla of Greek fishing boats escorted by Italian warships was disrupted by the Royal Navy. With tenuous control of the sea, British reinforcement was more successful. The battle quickly deteriorated into a struggle between German airpower and Italian naval forces versus Royal Navy seapower, and the isolated German parachutists were hard-pressed. On May 28 the Germans resorted to the expedient of beaching a cargo lighter and blowing the bow off with demolitions to land two light tanks. On the same day the Italian Navy managed to land a division unopposed. The British had already commenced a difficult evacuation of the island, though about 40 per cent of the British and most of the Greek forces were captured.

ASSESSMENT: British control of the sea and German control of the air resulted in a vicious tit-for-tat struggle, with airpower finally dominant. The attack nearly foundered because of Axis failure to achieve early dominance that would have allowed heavy forces to be introduced. Crete was an early example of the limited staying power of strictly airborne forces as opposed to heavier amphibious forces, a lesson that remains valid today.

Zapadnaya Litsa Bay, Arctic, July 14, 1941

In Operation *Barbarossa* Germany and its Finnish ally attacked on a broad front from the Black Sea to the Arctic Ocean. A prime goal was the strategically critical ice-free Arctic port of Murmansk. German lead elements established a beachhead on the eastern bank of the Zapadnaya Litsa River, so a Soviet tactical landing was conducted on July 6 to drive back the Germans. The landing was a total surprise, the Germans were pinned down by naval gunfire. At the same time the Soviet 52nd Infantry Division attacked from the east, and both units linked up and drove the Germans off the eastern bank. The next day a composite battalion of Russian sailors and soldiers landed on the western bank of the river. The Soviet beachhead was precarious, but it was a success in that the Germans lost offensive momentum.

A Germans counterattack on July 12 forced the Russians to abandon the western bank, but on July 14 a reinforced Soviet regiment landed on the western side of the river mouth, protected by ships and aircrafts, as a raid by 50 commandos conducted sabotage behind enemy lines. In two and a half hours the beachhead was established and troops were pushing westward.

On July 16, 700 additional sailors were landed to reinforce the regiment, but German troops drawn from other sectors were converging. Outnumbered and with insufficient artillery, the Soviets fell back. On the night of August 3 they withdrew on the eastern bank. The maneuver forced the Germans to move even more troops far from their main objectives to the south, but the Germans were still unable to cross the river and their offensive bogged down.

In late April of 1942 the Northern Fleet conducted another series of diversionary amphibious attacks in Motovskiy Bay to exhaust German troops and force them to finally abandon the Murmansk objective. Again, the landings were a total surprise. Destroyers dealt efficiently with German shore batteries, and by May 12 the Soviets occupied a beachhead seven miles deep and 10 miles wide. German counterattacks were numerically superior, and Soviet casualties mounted. Positions became untenable under German counterattacks and temperatures that even in spring regularly went below 0°C. On May 12 and 13 the Soviets evacuated their troops.

ASSESSMENT: The Soviets had successfully blunted the German drive on Murmansk. The German failure would later have immense effect on the outcome of the war as American weapons and supplies flooded in through Murmansk.

Estonia, September 18, 1941

Operation *Beowulf II* was the invasion of the Estonian islands of Saaremaa, Hiiumaa and Muhu that dominated the sea approaches to Leningrad. In Russian hands since annexation in June 1940, the garrison was composed of 20,000 troops with shore batteries concentrated on the shores of Saaremaa.

Beowulf I never materialized because of delays that German troops faced on the mainland, so they decided to pursue the *Beowulf II* plan to attack from the west coast of Estonia. A series of diversionary attacks were set up to confuse and divide the Russian defenders of Muhu. German naval forces would harass the southern and western shores of Saaremaa, and Germany's Finnish ally would undertake another diversionary attack against the shores of Hiiumaa.

The main assault would be protected by three cruisers, six floating artillery platforms, six coastal motor ships outfitted with *Sturmboot* (small boats with outboard motors designed for river crossings), 54 landing craft, and the transport *H-27*. The Finns contributed two coastal battleships and two icebreakers.

Prior to the main attack, the tiny islets of Vormsi, Hobulaiu and Kesse were seized on September 8–10. On September 13 Kriegsmarine and Finnish ships staged a diversion to lure Russian troops to the west. On September 14 a 15-minute preparatory bombardment on Muhu delivered by support ships and bombers was to clear beach obstacles and routes through minefields. Troops in the first wave of assault boats left the Estonian coast at

0450 hours, but dense fog and Russian fire delayed the approach. In the confusion some troops hit the wrong beaches. By noon only about half of the landing craft were still operable. The next day the Germans captured the rest of Muhu without resistance.

On September 16 the Germans attacked across a causeway and established advanced positions on Saaremaa after coastal batteries were neutralized by commandos. By early October 1941 Russian defenders were pressed down the Sworbe peninsula, south of Saaremaa Island. Trapped, they surrendered on October 5. It was now time for the Germans to undertake the invasion of Hiiumaa in a shore-to-shore landing from the northern coast of Saaremaa. On October 12 troops crossed the channel between the islands. German infantry met no opposition and quickly established a beachhead. Progress to the north was rapid as Russian troops began to evacuate the island. By October 21 the entire archipelago was in German hands.

Despite a rather disorganized landing on Muhu that could have ended badly for the Germans, the operation was a success, thanks to the demonstration forces off the coast of Saaremaa.

Grigorievka (Odessa), Black Sea, September 1941

During the siege of Odessa on the west coast of the Black Sea by the Romanian Army, the Soviets conducted a combined amphibious–airborne landing behind enemy lines to relieve pressure on the city. In the early hours of September 22, after a 30-minute preparatory bombardment from the supporting ships, about 2,000 Soviet Naval Infantry began landing on three beaches. At dawn *Stukas* sank a Soviet destroyer and damaged two more. Within a few hours Soviet troops established two beachheads but were repulsed from the third.

Planes transporting Soviet paratroopers dropped their loads six miles north of the beaches, creating more confusion in Romanian ranks, and linked up with the amphibious troops three miles inland. The joint force met forces advancing from Odessa, enlarging the port's defensive perimeter.

This tactical success allowed the Soviets to temporarily maintain the use of the harbor and pushed the Romanian artillery out of range, but the city eventually fell into Romanian hands on October 16.

Kertch-Feodossiya (Crimea), Black Sea, December 26, 1941

By December the Germans had besieged Sebastopol, a key port on the Black Sea. The Soviets planned a strategic landing to open a new front in German-held territory to relieve pressure around Sebastopol. Two armies totaling 60,000 men would undertake a shore-to-shore landing from the Taman Peninsula to the Kertch Peninsula. On the morning of December 26 a preliminary naval bombardment alerted the Germans of an incoming assault. The preparatory bombardment failed completely. German coastal batteries opened a deadly fire on the landing boats, but the attackers were too numerous. Despite the enormous chaos (boats could not move at the same speed), beachheads were established under constant German air and artillery attack. Simultaneously, paratroopers were dropped behind German lines to create more confusion.

ASSESSMENT: The overwhelming number of attackers made this operation a success. It forced the Germans to establish defensive positions on one side while 20 miles to the west, the siege of Sebastopol continued. This operation delayed the German capture of Sebastopol by six months.

From the summer of 1940 onward dozens of amphibious raids were directed against the coast of occupied France, reconnaissance and sabotage missions to gather information, and to perturb German defense systems and communication lines. These operations fulfilled one of the classic missions of amphibious raids: keeping the enemy off balance, forcing dispersion of effort to defend a long coastline, and above all providing a means for a weak force to harass and delay a stronger enemy.

Perhaps the most famous of them was Operation *Chariot*. This saw 600 British commandos and Royal Navy personnel storm the harbor of St. Nazaire during the night of March 27/28, 1942. The Normandie drydock at St. Nazaire was the only one on the Atlantic coast that could accommodate very large ships like the German battleship *Tirpitz* for repairs. The presence of this battleship in the Atlantic would threaten the viability of American convoys to Britain. If the Normandie drydock could be wrecked, the *Tirpitz* and German cruisers would be forced to make repairs at facilities in the Baltic, where they could be more easily bottled up by the Royal Navy.

HMS *Campbelltown*, an obsolete destroyer provided by the United States under the Lend-Lease program, was packed with explosives and rammed into the gates of the drydock. When the explosives were detonated by a time fuse, the explosion damaged the facility so badly that it was not fully repaired until 1950. Most of the supporting craft that were supposed to evacuate the raiders were sunk, and the surviving commandos captured.

The Dieppe Raid, August 12, 1942

By mid-1942, Stalin requested that the Allies open a new front to reduce the pressure on his troops fighting the Germans in the East. The Western Allies were far too weak to open a second front, but a major raid would help divert German forces from the east, and provide experience in a major amphibious operation to seize and briefly hold a port in northern France. Another idea behind this Operation *Jubilee* was to let the German think that the Allies would select an area in the Pas-de-Calais, close to England, to invade Europe and keep German attention focused on this point.

On August 12, 1942, 6,000 assault troops—for the most part Canadians—were landed to assault the beaches surrounding the harbor of Dieppe. The operation was supported by 74 squadrons of fighters and bombers from the Royal Air Force, but instead of concentrating the bombing on and immediately behind the objective, bombings were spread across vast areas and far inland, behind the objective.

When the first troops landed they were met by intense machine-gun fire. Preliminary operations east and west of the objective achieved their goals of destroying coastal gun emplacements, but also alerted the Germans that something was in the offing.

The tank support began landing too late, leaving the infantry alone on the beach. The fierce German resistance surprised the Canadians, who underestimated the number of defenders. Indeed, the Allied intelligence thought that only 500 troops were defending the harbor, while actually, nearly 4,000 were assigned the task of protecting Dieppe. The naval gunfire support was not powerful enough. The largest ships to support the operation were eight destroyers whose guns were unable to knock out the German bunkers.

The infantry could not benefit from artillery support: no artillery was planned to land. Adding to the confusion, most NCOs and Officers became casualties soon after landing. The inability of troops to take the initiative caused the operation to stall. Momentum was lost and the arrival of tanks didn't turn the tide of the operation. The nature of the ground was unknown to planners and caused many tanks to throw tracks on the pebble beaches. The constant flow of radio communications to the offshore ships led to miscommunications and misunderstandings. All this combined to allow the Germans to bring in reinforcements and increase the defense. Despite the large number of RAF planes in the sky, they were not master of it.

The raid was intended to capture and briefly hold the port, but after only five hours an evacuation was ordered amid the chaos. Casualties were high and morale dropped among the Allies, particularly the Canadians, who lost more than 2,800 men killed, wounded, taken prisoner, or missing. A large quantity of matériel, including all the tanks landed, was abandoned.

ASSESSMENT: The results of the operation were mixed. It surely taught the Allies about the critical points that needed to be improved before the opening of a new front in Western Europe, and contributed to the cancellation of Operation *Gymnast*, an ill-conceived plan for a 1942 invasion of France. Many analysts later questioned whether the knowledge gained was worth the sacrifice. It forced the Germans to concentrate defensive strength on the Atlantic Wall, releasing pressure on the Soviets. But it had the unintended consequence of alerting the Nazis to the vulnerability of their protective wall. Until the Normandy invasion the Germans worked tirelessly to improve coastal defenses and armament.

In addition to small raids along the Atlantic coast, the British continued to pick at the other edges of Occupied Europe and in other more remote regions. Operation *Abstention* was an invasion of the island of Kastelorizo, off the Turkish coast, in February 1941.

The Pacific

Japanese expansionism into Southeast Asia began with border clashes on September 6, 1940, and an amphibious landing near Haiphong on September 26 to seize French Indochina (modern-day Vietnam) from the Vichy French.

On December 7, 1941 numerous attacks had to be undertaken simultaneously, stretching Japanese assets to the limit. The main objectives were Singapore, Malaya, Hong Kong, the Dutch East Indies and the Philippines, but Japan's vulnerable eastern flank needed to be secured, hence the importance of Wake Island and Guam.

At this point Japanese doctrine was built around surprise, with reserve troops brought ashore in a second wave.

The first Japanese amphibious assault actually preceded the Pearl Harbor raid by about an hour. The British in Malaya had detected an invasion fleet, but hesitated to attack it for fear it was a provocation to start a war. Just after midnight local time Japanese infantry, light artillery, and engineers loaded into landing boats, but rough seas capsized several landing craft. At the beach the invaders encountered an Indian brigade dug in behind sturdy defenses. The first two landing waves were pinned down with heavy casualties, but the Japanese continued to push troops ashore. Suicidal attacks finally forced the Indians back. By December 10 the Japanese had captured the airfield complex at Kota Bharu, a first step in the conquest of Singapore.

In comparison, the successful Japanese effort against the US Territory of Guam on December 8–10 was gross overkill. The large island was defended by 547 American Marines and sailors, and the native Insular Guard Force (police) against 5,400 Rikusentai and Imperial Army infantry. A fleet of 20 warships and two transports opposed an American minesweeper and two small patrol boats. The large island fell within days.

Wake Island, December 11 – 23, 1941

A preliminary aerial bombardment began the same day as the Pearl Harbor attack, but the first Japanese attempt to land on the island was on December 11. Japanese doctrine emphasized surprise and landing at an undefended site, but neither was possible on the tiny islands of the Central Pacific. In addition, the invasion force was cobbled together, and the Rikusentai landed from ships' boats without any weapon heavier than a machine gun. There was no air support.

Forewarned by Japanese aerial reconnaissance, American Marines and Navy personnel relocated six five-inch guns for coastal defense. A problem for the Americans was that the doctrine for the Marine Corps Defense Battalions emphasized heavy weapons, but there was no infantry maneuver element to counterattack a landing.

The Japanese fleet approached the island, confident of surprise, and the defenders held fire until the ships were close to the beach. Accurate fire from the coastal guns threw the landing into complete disarray, even though any one of the nine Japanese gunfire support ships boasted more guns than the entire island. The Japanese fleet struggled to escape, pursued by four Marine Corps fighter planes. Two destroyers were sunk and a light cruiser badly damaged. The attackers had grossly underestimated the fighting capacities of the defenders and were not master of the skies.

The Japanese launched relentless bombing by land-based bombers. A second attempt on December 23 was reinforced by two aircraft carriers, more gunfire support ships, and another 1,500 Rikusentai. The exhausted defenders surrendered after a day-long fight on December 23, but the Japanese lost two converted destroyers used as landing ships, and some 28 planes.

ASSESSMENT: Japanese overconfidence, misguided reliance upon surprise, and lack of proper equipment resulted in the only amphibious assault in World War II to be completely defeated at the water's edge.

Manila Bay on the big island of Luzon in the Philippines was not only the best harbor in the region, but ships based there could dominate the sea lanes between Japan and the East Indies. The Japanese plan was not to attack the main American bases directly, but to land at Lingayen Gulf 135 miles to the north and attack overland.

The landings were disrupted by bad weather and ships lost their way, spreading the invasion force over a wide area. Landing boats were wrecked, and no heavy weapons could be landed. The landings succeeded only because of inadequate defense by untrained Filipino troops, and ineffective attacks by American submarines and bombers.

Following a protracted land campaign, the final act of the struggle for the Philippines was a Japanese shore-to-shore amphibious assault on Corregidor, the American island fortress that controlled entrance to Manila Bay. The Japanese bombed and shelled the island without letup for 66 days, and attacked on the evening of May 5, 1942. The defenders inflicted heavy losses, nearly annihilating one of the landing forces despite having only obsolete 37mm cannons as their heaviest weapons. During the night the Japanese tenaciously poured more forces ashore, including their heaviest tanks and captured American tanks. The starving and worn-out defenders surrendered the next day.

ASSESSMENT: The Philippines campaign, and particularly the amphibious assaults, had proven an embarrassment to the overconfident Japanese.

Timor, February 20, 1942

Timor was the gateway to Australia because of the presence of a deepwater harbor on the island, only 450 miles northwest of Australia. Preliminary bombing alerted the Australian and Dutch forces on the island that Timor was about to be attacked. In the predawn hours of February 20 the Japanese began disembarking forces on the western end of the island. The four beaches were undefended, and to preserve the surprise effect the Japanese didn't employ preliminary naval gunfire. Paratroopers were dropped behind Allied lines to prevent the defenders from withdrawing while the amphibious force was progressing inland. Another airdrop was conducted on the second day to reinforce the ground attackers. Hampered by poor communications and lack of heavy weapons, Australian and Dutch troops surrendered after heroic resistance.

ASSESSMENT: With control of both the air and sea, the Timor operation provided a much better example of what a combined airborne–amphibious operation could achieve than had Crete. Though little-known, Timor would serve as a template in which light airborne forces disrupted the defense and isolated the battle space while heavier amphibious forces delivered the main blow.

The Japanese conducted numerous other amphibious operations, mostly unopposed, as they conquered European colonies like Hong Kong, the remainder of the Dutch East Indies, and the minor islands of the Central Pacific. One of their most significant operations was little-noticed at the time, but would lead to some of the worst fighting of the war. Newly appointed American General Douglas MacArthur ignored naval intelligence reports that the Japanese were planning operations against the north coast of New Guinea, with an eye toward crossing the high and rugged Owen Stanley Mountains to capture strategic Port Moresby, a gateway to northern Australia. As a result the Japanese landings at Gona on July 21, 1942 were observed but unopposed, and a beachhead quickly established. The Japanese were able to advance rapidly and six months of bitter fighting by Australian and American forces would be required to dislodge the enemy.

The Japanese rampage finally staggered to a stop for the same reasons many nations had experienced over the centuries: the extension of their communication lines made further gains impossible and their initial gains untenable. The power of the United States was beginning to make itself felt, and Japanese expansion was blunted in the battle of the Coral Sea (May 1942). In June 1942 the Japanese attempted to lure the American fleet into a trap at the battle of Midway. One quite unnecessary component of the plan was the invasion of the Aleutian islands of Attu and Kiska to lure American naval forces northward. Instead, Japan suffered a stunning naval defeat. The final blow was the complete destruction of a Japanese invasion fleet in the battle of the Bismarck Sea, near New Guinea in March 1943.

Japanese industrial capacity was increasingly devoted to replacement of planes, battleships, and aircraft carriers. Nevertheless the Imperial forces continued to develop innovative vessels.

Despite their deteriorating strategic situation, the Japanese were well ahead of the Americans in developing a practical **amphibious light tank**, the Type 2 *Ka-Mi*. Equipped with large flotation tanks fore and aft of the main hull, it could be driven up onto the beach and the flotation tanks jettisoned. The Americans would deploy a similar but more sophisticated system in 1945.

The most interesting were the Navy's 21 destroyer-sized T.1 fast transports, built in 1944–1945. Five preloaded landing craft or seven Ka-Mi amphibious tanks could be winched up onto rails on the sloping rear deck. At the objective the ship ballasted down at the stern, and the tanks/boats were cast loose to slide down into the water while the ship was under way and less vulnerable to attack.

In 1943 the Imperial Army accepted a single strange hybrid ship that was the predecessor of an entirely new class of amphibious transport. The *Shinshū Maru* had a huge boxy superstructure that could accommodate 25–29 landing barges and 20 small seaplanes. Preloaded Daihatsu could be quickly launched by sliding down rails.

Belatedly the Imperial forces also began to cooperate more closely in the development and construction of specialized amphibious vessels. The Germans provided Japan with information on the Allied landing craft used in North Africa, and from this the Imperial services developed two types of large mechanized landing craft. Six of the No. 101 class vessels were built in 1944, and the more common type was the No. 103, but with only 69 built between 1943 and 1945. These were seagoing craft capable of landing seven medium tanks, 13–14 light tanks, or seven of the bulky Ka-Mi.

By the time the T.1 and No. 101/103 vessels entered service the period of Japanese offensives was long past. Most were sunk while serving as supply carriers in attempts to support isolated garrisons. For the remainder of the war Japanese amphibious operations would be limited to pinprick tactical landings, minor attempts to outflank Allied landing positions.

CHAPTER 7

≈≈≈≈≈≈≈≈≈≈≈≈≈≈≈≈≈≈≈

THE WAR IN THE PACIFIC

Even before the debacle at Midway measures were being taken to blunt Japanese expansion. On Easter Sunday, April 5, 1942 the Japanese struck at Colombo on Ceylon (modern Sri Lanka) in a surprise raid intended to force the Royal Navy out of the eastern Indian Ocean. The Japanese struck Trincomalee harbor four days later, sinking a British aircraft carrier and two escort vessels. The Royal Navy decided to relocate its fleet base to Kenya.

Madagascar, May 5–6, 1942

In the early months of 1942 the Japanese seemed invincible. To prevent them from gaining a foothold in the western Indian Ocean, the British decided to capture Madagascar from the French Collaborationist Government. At dawn on May 5 British commandos landed in the northwestern coast to spearhead Operation *Ironclad*. Their objective was a coastal defense battery atop a ridge dominating the landing beaches.

The surprise was total since the French assumed the beach was protected by a reef, but a breach in the reef was found by the Royal Navy, allowing its ships to enter the small lagoon. In the nearby harbor of Diego Suarez a French "colonial cruiser" poured accurate fire on the assault troops until it was silenced the next day.

During the night of May 5/6 fifty Royal Marines landed on the east of the peninsula to seize dominating French positions there. With a beachhead firmly established, a land campaign began that ended with the Vichy surrender on November 6.

ASSESSMENT: Fortunately for the British, the Vichy French did not expect a landing and did not defend the beaches.

The Pacific Theater, 1942–1945

By early 1942 the Japanese were threatening communications routes to Australia, and threatened Samoa, a key base for any future offensive. On August 7/8, 1942 the 1st Marine Division landed to recapture Guadalcanal. The attackers first landed on surrounding islets, particularly Tanambogo. Landings on the small islands met with fierce resistance, but on Guadalcanal the Japanese withdrew into the jungle.

Despite all their planning the landings on the main island were chaotic. Troops milled about and supplies piled up on the beach. In the face of any opposition the landing would have been disastrous.

On the night of August 8/9 the Japanese sent a fleet of cruisers and a destroyer in a night attack, the nightmare scenario for any amphibious landing. They sank three American cruisers, an Australian cruiser, and damaged other Allied vessels, but failed to attack the vulnerable transports. The Navy operational commander decided to send the fleet to safety. The Marines were left on their own, most of their supplies and heavy equipment still aboard the transports.

The survival of the Marines on Guadalcanal was largely due to food and fuel left behind by the Japanese, and to Japanese disorganization. The landings opened a six-month-long jungle, air, and sea struggle.

ASSESSMENT: Serious operational problems surfaced, particularly as critical equipment and supplies were not landed during first few hours of the operation. Moreover, Americans and their allies were unable to dominate the skies and waters around Guadalcanal, leaving troops ashore without adequate support for a prolonged period.

The logistics of early amphibious landings in World War II were chaotic, even when unopposed. This period pre-dated packaged combat rations, and some boxes are labeled "Rice Krispies" cereal™ and "DO NOT WET". (National Archives)

American weakness in the early days of the war led them to create raiding forces patterned after the British commandos. The Marine Corps units were two Raider battalions. On the night of August 17/18 the 2nd Raider Battalion attacked Makin Atoll in the Gilbert Islands, to help disperse Japanese efforts. The small Japanese garrison was annihilated, but the raid had terrible unintended consequences. The Japanese were alerted to the vulnerability of their scattered island outposts and began to concentrate forces on more defensible islands.

Far to the north, American and Canadian troops attacked to recover Attu in the Aleutian Islands on May 11, 1943. The garrison took to the hills. The brief campaign culminated in disorganized Japanese counterattacks and mass suicides on May 29. On August 15 the Allies invaded Kiska, only to discover that the Japanese had evacuated the island.

Following Guadalcanal a dispute surfaced between the two primary American commanders, General Douglas MacArthur and

Admiral Chester Nimitz, over whether priority was to be granted to a Southwest Pacific offensive to liberate the Philippines and the long-planned Central Pacific drive. In the end, it was apparent that American resources allowed two offensives, nullifying any Japanese advantage gained from interior lines of communication. Two drives would keep the Japanese under continuous left–right blows. It was anticipated that the two would converge at Formosa (modern Taiwan).

The Southwest Pacific, 1942–1945

Even before the end at Guadalcanal the Allies commenced other operations to roll back the Japanese. In early May a Japanese invasion fleet bound for eastern New Guinea was defeated at the battle of the Coral Sea, and efforts by the Japanese to attack Port Moresby, New Guinea by land had been repulsed. A small Japanese force was stranded on Goodenough Island, northeast of New Guinea, when their boats were destroyed by Allied aircraft. On October 22 Australian forces landed in Operation *Drake*, forcing a Japanese evacuation.

The Allied drive through the Solomon Islands, the reconquest of New Guinea, and the return to the Philippines is notable in that it was not the individual battles that were significant, but the cumulative amphibious strategy. While battles were no less savage

General of the Army Douglas MacArthur made masterful use of amphibious landings to bypass centers of Japanese resistance in the Southwest Pacific. His campaigns produced perhaps the greatest strategic result with the lowest cost in Allied lives of any in World War II. His plan for the 1950 Inchon invasion in Korea is considered the greatest amphibious assault in history. (National Archives)

than in other theaters, on a grander scale MacArthur adopted a variation of the prewar strategy of the indirect approach, but instead of landing and marching to battle, the Allies would land and forge a ring of new bases around major objectives.

Operation *Cartwheel* was MacArthur's long-term plan for a series of attacks to isolate and neutralize the Japanese garrisons. Overall it was to be a masterful campaign to bypass and isolate Japanese strongholds in a battle of engineers. On the grander scale, Allied strategy would be to land at numerous relatively undefended sites and quickly construct new airfields. The huge Japanese base at Rabaul on New Britain was to be isolated by landings to fence in the large Japanese garrison, leaving them to starve. Simultaneously, the Americans and Australians would clear the north coast of New Guinea to secure the left flank of a greater advance on the Philippines.

The seizures of Woodlark and Kirimina islands (Operation *Chronicle*, June 25–30, 1943) were uncontested. Then the offensive took an inexplicable misdirection. The initial stage of *Cartwheel* did not go at all well when MacArthur moved against New Georgia (Operation *Toenails*, June 20–October 7, 1943). There the American Army command decided not to move directly against a major Japanese base at Munda. In the planned offensive the Americans would adhere to a cherished but obsolete strategy—the indirect approach then much in vogue among military theoreticians. This consisted of landing at an undefended point and moving overland. The first landings were at the far end of the island, nearly 40 miles from the main objective. The advance immediately bogged down in dense jungle, and required a series of new landings to establish new beachheads closer to the final objective. The new plan was overly complex, with multiple landings at separate and not mutually supporting beachheads. The Americans established positions on Rendova Island to shell the main Japanese position, and Marine Raiders were landed in a dense mangrove swamp at isolated Bairoko in an effort to sever enemy supply lines.

The thick rain forest prevented adequate tank support, the supply chain was not continuous due to the muddy trails, Japanese defenses were difficult to locate in the jungle, aerial support was ineffective,

The naval situation off **New Georgia** deteriorated into incessant enemy air attacks, and nocturnal battles in restricted waters. With control of both the sea and air contested, losses of planes and ships were high, including the attack transport USS *McCawley*, and the obscure *PT109* commanded by Lieutenant (j.g.) John F. Kennedy.

and weather conditions, disease, and an unusually high incidence of psychiatric casualties debilitated the American troops. The ensuing jungle combat lasted for more than three months until the area commander, Admiral William Halsey, decided enough was enough. Planned landings on the next island in the chain were canceled. The strategy of indirect approach was quietly abandoned.

The next landings at Cape Torokina on Bougainville (Operation *Cherryblossom*) turned the New Georgia experience on its head. The Japanese had constructed large bases at the ends of the island. In coordination with a diversionary operation against Choiseul Island to the east, the 3rd Marine Division landed at Empress Augusta Bay and immediately began construction of airfields. This time the Japanese were forced to struggle through 50 miles of horrific jungle to attack the American position.

The capture of Arawe (Operation *Director*, December 15, 1943) was primarily a diversion to support landings at Cape Gloucester on New Britain (Operation *Dexterity*, January 2, 1944), on the opposite end of the big island from Rabaul. The landings at Cape Gloucester were for all practical purposes unopposed, but followed by a protracted jungle campaign. With relatively limited resources, the American Marines made use of small shore-to-shore landings to outflank the Japanese, supported by improvised weapons like light observation planes fitted with "bazooka" rocket launchers, and tanks carried in landing craft as improvised gunboats.

The Admiralty Islands were thought to be lightly defended, and, on February 29, 1944 the US Army landed unopposed (Operation *Brewer*). Intelligence was faulty, the islands strongly garrisoned, and the fighting dragged on until May 18.

The northern New Guinea campaign commenced with the effort to isolate the entire Japanese 18th Army at Wewak. Operation *Persecution*, a landing at Altape and the main landings near the port of Hollandia (Operation *Reckless*) began badly when the landing force at Tanhamera Bay found itself penned in by impassable swamps. The main landing force was quickly redirected to Humboldt Bay, where the Japanese fled into the jungle. An unusually fierce battle to reduce the original Japanese position at Buna-Gona resulted in horrific Japanese losses and a resort to cannibalism when supply lines were severed. It ended with one of the few, relatively successful, Japanese amphibious evacuations of a handful of survivors.

Operation *Hurricane* (May 27–August 17, 1944) was a grinding three-month struggle for the large island of Biak, off northern New Guinea. The Japanese initiated a new strategy of not contesting the Allied landings, but to bog the Allies down in jungle fighting. On July 30 Allied forces landed on the Vogelkop Peninsula, the extreme northwestern tip of New Guinea, and offshore islands (Operation *Typhoon*) where they quickly constructed airfields.

With New Guinea and the Solomons secured, and Rabaul neutralized, by late 1943 Allied forces had hammered Japanese forces in the southwest Pacific to near total collapse. Planning for future operations had to be modified on the fly. The original plan for the liberation of the Philippines called for landings on Mindanao as a prelude to the main attack on Leyte. A fast carrier attack on island chains east of Mindanao, primarily the Palaus, was to be the prelude to the capture of the islands to remove the threat of attack against the rear of the main invasion force. But by mid-1944 Japanese forces on Peleliu were no longer a credible threat and Nimitz suggested that the Palaus be bypassed. When the attack indicated that Japanese strength in the Palau Islands was minimal, it was decided to bypass Mindanao.

Misgivings over authority, chain of command, and operational boundaries led to one of the tragedies of the Pacific war. MacArthur was under radio silence en route to the Philippines. Nimitz felt that he did not have authority to cancel Operation *Stalemate II* that had been mounted to support MacArthur's landings. Army landings on Angaur were lightly opposed, but the Peleliu landings on September 15 were followed by one of the most brutal—and futile—battles of the Pacific war.

Reconnaissance was faulty. Judging by the smoothness of the tree canopy, the planners concluded that the island was flat, but the island was actually cut by steep ravines and high cliffs. The trees had grown taller in the ravines than on the heights, creating an illusion. Worse, manpower and equipment were limited; the allocated tank strength was reduced by a third because of lack of ships to carry them.

The Japanese contested the landings, but then began a savage two-month battle of attrition in which they had to be rooted out of interconnected subterranean defenses. The greatest prize fell into American hands unopposed on September 23 when Army troops landed on Falalop Island. The lagoon at Ulithi Atoll was one of the finest anchorages in the western Pacific, and became a major staging base for future operations.

ASSESSMENT: The battle for Peleliu was the first large-scale application of the Japanese tactic of lightly defending the beaches, instead burrowing below ground for a major battle of attrition, a tactic that would achieve its highest level at Iwo Jima and Okinawa. Nimitz's failure to cancel the Peleliu operation under his own authority proved highly controversial.

The invasion of the large landmasses of the Philippines marked a transition to a more conventional war in which amphibious operations created the doorway for the US Army to engage in conventional land combat. The invasion was quite complex, with multiple supporting operations, including landings to secure small islands east of the main island of Leyte on October 17.

The main landing of Operation *King II* was actually two landings on widely separated beaches on the eastern side of Leyte. The plan was for one force to sweep north, the other south, to quickly clear Japanese resistance. The landings were so successful that by afternoon over 132,000 troops were ashore, hindered more by swamps than the enemy. Unfortunately the land offensive met stiffening Japanese resistance and mountainous terrain, forcing transport and support ships to linger longer than expected. Leyte also witnessed a major Japanese air and naval counteroffensive, the battle of Leyte Gulf, once the greatest fear of amphibious planners. In one of the largest naval battles in history, Japanese losses in ships and planes proved prohibitive. Desperate attempts to attack the American fleet off Leyte marked the first appearance of Japanese *kamikaze* suicide air attacks.

The ability of the Japanese Army to resist landings had virtually disappeared, and the large island of Mindoro was quickly captured. Little hindered a massive landing on the main island of Luzon, where 175,000 men went ashore along a broad 20-mile beachhead. The final act was the invasion of Palawan on February 28, 1945, against very weak resistance, followed by landings on several smaller islands (Operations *Victor III*, *IV* and *V*).

OVERALL ASSESSMENT: MacArthur's amphibious strategy of "hitting 'em where they ain't" was overall the most successful of the war. Enormous strategic results and massive enemy casualties from starvation and disease were achieved with minimal Allied losses: the entire campaign resulted in fewer Allied casualties than in the German Ardennes offensive of December 1944.

The Central Pacific, 1942–1945

The first amphibious assault, a frontal attack from the sea, would be at Betio Island on Tarawa Atoll, in the Gilbert Islands. Carlson's 1942 raid prompted the Japanese to relocate primary facilities to smaller, more defensible islands, primarily in the Gilbert Islands (Betio Island, Tarawa Atoll) and Marshall Islands (Roi-Namur, Kwajalein Atoll). The taking of Tarawa was judged necessary because the airstrip located on Betio could host bombers to help reduce defenses in the Marshall Islands.

Aerial photographs allowed the planners to determine the number of defenders thanks to the latrines built around Betio. Knowing the standard number of troops per latrine, they were able to determine with incredible precision the number of Japanese defenders. The Americans decided to use LVT logistics vehicles as assault vehicles to cross the reef surrounding the island.

On November 20, 1943 the preliminary aerial and naval bombardment failed to silence the coastal artillery positions. LVTs carrying the first waves were delayed because of their slow speed, and when the naval bombardment ceased the planes supposed to commence bombing were nowhere to be seen. This respite gave the Japanese time to reorganize their defense. The planes finally appeared, but the dust and smoke prevented further support because of the risk of friendly fire.

The LVTs reached the shore and landed the first troops under a hail of gunfire. Following waves were loaded into boats, but were unable to cross the reef. Troops had to disembark in up to five feet of water under intense fire.

For the first time a specialized ship was used to bring preloaded tank lighters. The Landing Ship Dock (LSD) USS *Ashland*, another of Roland Baker's designs, was able to carry preloaded LCMs. The ship was equipped with a stern gate that was opened once the ship had ballasted down to release the landing craft. Medium tanks landed 20 minutes after the first troops, but light tanks were loaded in the bottom of the holds, and could not be disembarked when critically needed.

On the main landing beach only a single undamaged radio made it ashore, but could not communicate with other beachheads. The Marines expected a Japanese counterattack on the first night, which never materialized. The situation was saved when infantry and a single surviving tank helped to clear one landing beach, allowing the Americans to bring intact infantry units ashore.

After 72 hours of unusually savage combat, the island was finally secured. The rest of the atoll fell in the following days, without resistance.

Makin was far less staunchly defended, but there the situation was reversed. Army troops achieved a lightly opposed landing and conducted a slow and methodical attack. The Japanese were in part able to conduct a *yogaki*, a naval counterattack on the ships offshore. A submarine succeeded in sinking the light aircraft carrier USS *Liscome Bay*, with heavier loss of life than in the fighting ashore.

ASSESSMENT: The assaults on Tarawa and Makin were the first in many regards, and taught invaluable lessons to the Allies in the ways of amphibious warfare. Far better intelligence and reconnaissance was required. At Tarawa bungled loading, the rush to set troops ashore and have the transports depart, and the chaos among the landing force, resulted in acts like toilet paper being sent ashore before desperately-needed ammunition for tanks. Tarawa might have been a complete disaster had the Japanese mounted a counterattack on the first night. Medium tanks provided much-needed support for the infantry, vindicating the emphasis placed on development of capabilities for landing tanks. Their 75mm guns were the only ones able to efficiently deal with Japanese fortifications. The loss of *Liscome Bay* reinforced the idea that a landing needed to be concluded as quickly as possible, even with higher losses among the landing force, to reduce the risk to ships standing offshore. Only 66 Americans were killed on Butaritari, 1,009 on Tarawa, and 687 (nearly 40 percent of total killed) in the sinking of *Liscome Bay*.

By early 1944, the front line had moved to the Marshall Islands, from where the large Japanese base on Truk could be isolated by American airpower. Though stiff resistance was anticipated, the assault on the main Japanese base on Roi-Namur proved to be brief (February 1/2) though conducted by a novice Marine division. A tactic that would be used in the future was to emplace artillery, more accurate than naval gunfire, on nearby undefended islands. The most notable problem was that some units advanced too quickly, with potential for being struck by preplanned naval gunfire.

The larger island of Kwajalein was assaulted by US Army forces; there the Japanese could not defend all the beaches, deciding instead to launch suicidal *banzai* counterattacks. The reduction of the smaller islands (Operation *Catchpole*) included an unparalleled feast of amphibious mobility. Forces in small landing craft traversed 28 miles of ocean to conduct three shore-to-shore landings in five days.

The capture of Kwajalein left four major Japanese atoll bases in the southeastern Marshalls, as well as Wake Island to the north, isolated as self-managed prisons.

American amphibious forces were now hitting their stride. Rather than ineffective naval area bombardment, targets were located by intense reconnaissance. Navy underwater demolition teams scouted beaches and blew up obstacles. Previous operations had used phase lines, recognizable terrain features at which the attacking forces would pause to avoid friendly fire incidents. Now radio-equipped Marine Corps and Navy teams would accompany the troops to coordinate naval gunfire and air attacks as needed.

Logistics have long been the bane of military operations, arguably more so for amphibious operations than for any other. By mid-1944 a host of innovations were revolutionizing amphibious logistics. Prepackaged foods, the famous C-rations, meant that it was no longer necessary to bring in bulk foods to be prepared in field kitchens (though a hot meal was a great morale-booster). Special Shore Party units had refined their craft so that fuel and supplies moved swiftly ashore. One of the unsung major weapons of the war was the bulldozer; Shore Party and Engineer units were equipped with bulldozers, cranes, and other heavy equipment, not just for construction but handling heavy cargo.

Roller conveyors meant that bulky or heavy cargo could be slid ashore without being carried on men's backs. Bulk fuel remained a problem, and a simple but important innovation was the barrel corral. Steel drums were partially filled with fuel and dumped into the sea off the beach, held in place by floating nets. When fuel was needed a boat was sent out to collect the requisite number of floating drums.

One problem that could not be resolved was the necessity of "push logistics." Needs for ammunition, fuel, food, and other commodities had to be planned in advance, based on prior experience. This was the origin of the famous "unit of fire," the anticipated ammunition needs of a unit in combat for one day. Upon arrival at the objective, supplies were "pushed" ashore, but problems of unanticipated needs for certain ammunition or supplies persisted.

By June 1944, the Americans were assaulting the Marianas (Operation *Forager*), beginning with Saipan, a Japanese protectorate since 1919. Compared to Tarawa the beaches were lightly defended, but the Japanese had placed ranging markers offshore to increase the accuracy of defensive fire. After a two-day bombardment two Marine divisions landed on June 15, and secured a beachhead despite a counterattack spearheaded by the largest Japanese tank force encountered during the war. Army troops were ashore the

General Holland M. "Howling Mad" Smith was the commander of the joint Army-Marine V Amphibious Corps, and later the Fleet Marine Force, Pacific. He is regarded as the "godfather" of modern amphibious doctrine. (Marine Corps History Division)

next day, and despite a massive *banzai* attack on July 7, the three divisions secured the island by July 9.

Saipan was marred by an incident that had long-term repercussions. The operational commander, Marine General Holland Smith, frustrated by the slow advance of the Army's 27th Division, relieved the commander, Major General Ralph Smith. The incident poisoned Army–Marine relations for over a half-century when army generals decreed that no major army formations would serve under Marine Corps command.

The final objective, Guam, had special significance for the American Marines. A US territory, it held the largest population of captive American civilians in the war; the small Marine constabulary force there had been overwhelmed in 1941.

The configuration of the coast was a major obstacle. The high and rugged Orote Peninsula dominated landing beaches to the north and south, and on July 21 guns there wreaked havoc on the attacking Marines. Casualties among the Army's 77th Division that landed in the afternoon south of (and closest to) the Orote Peninsula were even greater: lacking LVTs, they had to wade ashore under heavy fire. By July 25 the peninsula was isolated, and by July 29 the two beachheads were joined. The island was declared secure on August 10. Guam became a major submarine base for the blockade and strangulation of Japan.

The July 24 shore-to-shore assault on nearby Tinian has been called the most perfect amphibious assault in history. Precision bombardment was provided by artillery based on Saipan. Unit commanders conducted pre-invasion reconnaissance in person,

"Doodlebugs" were improvised engineer assault vehicles used to surmount low cliffs on Tinian. The forward ends of the steel beams were secured to the top of the cliff. When the vehicle backed away, large wooden beams connected by chains dropped into place to form a ramp. (National Archives)

flying above the future battlefield and peering down through the open bomb bay doors of Navy torpedo bombers.

An elaborate feint drew Japanese forces to the best landing beaches near Tinian town on the southwest coast. Instead the Marines landed on two small beaches the Japanese thought unsuitable because of the low cliffs near the water's edge. LVTs were fitted with an H-shaped frame, with heavy wooden beams connected by chains carried atop the vehicle. When the "doodlebugs" approached the cliffs, the upper, leading edges of the frame were anchored in place by assault engineers. As the vehicles backed away, the frame was released and dropped into position, and the beams slid off to form the decking for a ramp. Infantry and light vehicles quickly surmounted the cliffs.

Tinian was a plateau that allowed extensive use of tanks, in close coordination with aerial support and infantry. Tinian, captured at minimal cost, was developed into a huge "island aircraft carrier" for B-29 strategic bombers, and it was from there that the nuclear strikes on Hiroshima and Nagasaki were launched.

The Japanese naval effort to counterattack the beachheads led to the battle of the Philippine Sea where they lost three aircraft carriers, and over 60 aircraft and their crews. The losses were irreplaceable, and Japanese airpower virtually annihilated.

The DUKW amphibious truck was a major innovation, capable of carrying supplies from ships directly to inland supply dumps. With minor modifications, howitzers could be carried in the cargo compartment. (National Archives)

ASSESSMENT: By the time of the Marianas campaign specialized equipment like armored and cannon-armed LVTs, and DUKW amphibious trucks were available in adequate numbers. The Marines were growing more proficient at logistics and beachhead organization. The Army had by this time become the larger practitioner of amphibious warfare, with its own fleets of both troop carrying and cannon-armed LVTs. The larger land masses required a seamless transition from amphibious to conventional warfare, a skill quickly mastered by both services. The campaign also saw the first use of mechanized columns of tanks and LVTs in the Central Pacific.

The next step was securing Iwo Jima, an island located midway between Japan and the Marianas. Damaged bombers on their way back to the Marianas needed a safe place to land, the island hosted a radar station that gave the Japanese two hours warning of any oncoming raid, and American fighter aircraft based there could accompany and protect the big bombers.

Two Marine divisions, with a third to follow later, assaulted the island on February 19, 1945 (Operation *Detachment*). Japanese tactics had again changed. The new strategy was to let the attackers land, only to pour massive and deadly artillery fire on them; the

Japanese would have a large artillery force directed by a central fire-control center. Attackers faced an elaborate defense in depth, with pillboxes and caves connected by manmade tunnels.

The Americans had also grown far more sophisticated, with new equipment like oceangoing landing craft that eliminated the need for mother ships to transport and launch smaller beaching craft. The landing force also included sufficient dozer tanks, considerable engineer equipment, and even two flail tanks to clear landmines. They were able to quickly bring sufficient artillery, tanks, and supplies ashore despite the chaos on the beach. The onshore battle then turned into an exceptionally bloody battle of attrition.

ASSESSMENT: Casualties on Iwo Jima were the heaviest of the Pacific War, and it was the first battle where American casualties outnumbered Japanese losses. Iwo had no significant harbor to capture, but the Marines had finally mastered at least some of the logistical lessons needed to support a multidivisional landing force over open beaches. Divisions were reorganized for greater efficiency,

One would never imagine from this beach scene at Iwo Jima that by 1945 beachhead logistics were a fine art. Visible are various tractors, a DUKW, amphibious tractors, and a crane. The tractor at left is towing a Kiska sled, a wooden platform with skids to move heavy cargo over soft sand. At right of center is a large color-coded cloth beach marker. The man beside it is leaning on pole-mounted loudspeakers used to relay orders. (Marine Corps History Division)

The requirements of amphibious warfare led to many vehicles designed for other purposes being pressed into service. This M29 Weasel Arctic rescue vehicle is carrying Stokes liters for the wounded. (National Archives)

including more engineer and armored assets, special separate LVT battalions to make more efficient use of the limited number of LVTs, and concentration of transport and heavy artillery at corps level.

Okinawa was the first island belonging to the Japanese homeland to be assaulted (Operation *Iceberg*). Six divisions were landed on April 1, 1945, encountering no resistance. The Japanese now knew the Americans now had the firepower to crush any beach defense. The only thing that could be done was to let the Americans ashore and then inflict heavy casualties in the hope of forcing the Americans into a negotiated peace.

Okinawa was also the first use by the Americans of tanks fitted with the experimental T-6 Flotation Device, pontoons attached to the tank that could be jettisoned by explosive bolts. It was a far more sophisticated version of previous efforts by the Germans and Japanese. This allowed the tanks to land under their own power, minimizing the use of landing craft that were always in short supply.

Although Okinawa was a massive assault landing, second only to Normandy, the campaign was largely a land battle. The protracted battle did, however, force the US Navy to have supply and support vessels remain in position and vulnerable to attack. The Japanese made far more extensive use of *kamikaze* attacks, but there was nothing to be done to avoid this aerial *yogaki*.

Southeast Asia and The East Indies, 1945

By late April 1945 British and Indian troops were closing in on Rangoon. Unaware of the collapsing Japanese resistance, the Allies planned Operation *Dracula*, an amphibious assault on Rangoon. The city was bombed and Gurkhas were parachuted in to secure shore batteries that might resist movement up the Rangoon River. On May 2 landings began on both banks of the river, with plans for a major force to move upriver and attack the city proper. No opposition was encountered; the Japanese had evacuated the city.

By May 1945 Borneo, once a major source of oil for Japan, was isolated. Under British direction the Australians planned landings at multiple sites, collectively called Operation *Oboe*, though only three actually took place. Later condemned as a waste of lives and resources, the various landings and land campaign (May 1–August 15) did serve to liberate POWs from Japanese captivity. The culmination of the campaign was the last amphibious landing of the war, the capture of the oil production center at Balikpapan on July 1 (*Oboe II*).

An amphibious campaign, Operation *Zipper*, was planned for the recapture of Singapore, but the Japanese surrender resulted in cancellation.

The End in The Pacific, 1945

The invasion of the main islands of Japan was planned for early November 1945. Fourteen divisions totaling 450,000 men were to be used to assault 35 beaches on the south coast of Kyushu, dwarfing the Normandy landings. On August 6 and 9, 1945, atomic bombs were dropped on Hiroshima and Nagasaki.

At the Yalta conference in February 1945 Roosevelt and Churchill had urged Stalin to enter the fight against Japan. Stalin considered the request, and after the Germans surrendered in May 1945 the Soviets began to reorient some of their troops to the east.

The process was accelerated after the Americans dropped the first atomic bomb. Stalin knew he had to enter the fight if he desired to be part of the peace negotiations with Japan. On August 9 Soviet divisions swarmed over the Japanese garrisons in Manchuria, abrogating the neutrality pact established between both nations in 1941.

On August 15 Japan surrendered. Ignoring this fact, on August 18 the Soviets began a series of landings in the Kurile archipelago. Even though little resistance was met, the Soviets targeted civilians and ignored truce flags in their race through the Kuriles.

Simultaneously, the southern part of Sakhalin Island (in Japan's hands since the 1905 Russo-Japanese war) was attacked by ground and seaborne troops. On August 16 some 1,400 Soviet Naval Infantry undertook a shore-to-shore landing in the harbor of Toro and overwhelmed about 200 defenders. On August 20 a similar operation was conducted on the Maoka harbor but was strongly opposed.

The ultimate objective was the city of Yuzhno-Sakhalinsk. Soviet troops converged on the objective by ground, while paratroopers were dropped into the city outskirts to speed its capture. The island fell to the Russians on August 25, and troops massed in the south to invade the small islands east of Hokkaido Island. The fighting for these islands (though poorly defended) lasted until September 5.

It was already agreed that the Japanese-ruled Korean Peninsula would be arbitrarily divided into Soviet and American occupation zones at the 38th Parallel of latitude. The Soviets executed a series of small tactical landings to bypass token Japanese resistance, and quickly arrive at the dividing line.

CHAPTER 8

PICKING AT THE EDGES: NORTH AFRICA AND THE MEDITERRANEAN

"The enemy will be compelled to react to the threat of his communications and rear, and advantage must be taken of this to break through his main defences ..."

British General Sir Harold R. L. G. Alexander, speaking of the Anzio landing

Italy's inept adventurism drew Germany into unwanted commitments in the Balkans and North Africa. Though most histories concentrate on armored warfare in North Africa (though most of the fighting was done by infantry), there were a number of amphibious raids, most of which did not materially contribute to the campaigns. Primary among the reasons for failure were overly complex operational plans, poor weather prediction, and inadequate intelligence and reconnaissance.

Operation *Agreement* (September 24, 1942) was part of a grandiose plan intended to destroy German facilities and stores around Tobruk. The landings were badly botched: guides could not set up guide beacons on the beach, troops landed on the wrong beaches, and Italian and German resistance was heavy. As the landing force withdrew the Germans pressed home aerial and naval attacks. The British lost nearly 1,400 men killed or captured, with a cruiser, two destroyers, and several smaller vessels sunk. Axis losses were 16 killed and 50 wounded.

Operation *Flipper* was mounted to support a major British land offensive, Operation *Crusader*. The raid had multiple objectives, but was unique in that one objective was rumored to be to kill or capture one man—Erwin Rommel (no official records support this). On the night of November 14/15, 1941 members of No. 11 (Scottish) Commando landed from a submarine 250 miles behind German lines to rendezvous with members of the Long Range Desert Group (LRDG) who had moved overland. The situation deteriorated almost immediately. Bad weather prevented most of the commandos from landing. On the second night native guides refused to budge. The commandos had to climb the 1800-foot coastal escarpment and then march 16 miles through a storm to a hide near the objective.

Just before midnight on November 17 the commandos attacked what was believed to be Rommel's headquarters, but it was a complete fiasco. Not only had Rommel moved his headquarters elsewhere, but he was in Rome arguing for more support. The commandos attacked the quartermaster headquarters that now occupied the villa, only to be driven off when the operational commander was killed and his deputy gravely wounded. Many of the commandos were captured, and others scattered when the surf proved too rough to make it back to the submarine.

Operation *Torch*, November 8, 1942

The US Army had undertaken a crash amphibious warfare training program in Chesapeake Bay of the eastern United States, an area that could be secured against German U-boat attacks. The Army, with overwhelming manpower and resources, quickly became the foremost practitioners of the doctrine that Pete Ellis and others had developed.

The Soviets were desperately pressing the Western Allies to open a new front. The US Army argued for an invasion of Western Europe in 1942, but in British eyes this was impossible. The result was a compromise. Europe was abandoned in favor of North Africa, less well-defended, and in the hands of the weak French Collaborationist Government. The 125,000 defending troops had low morale and were equipped with a mix of weapons, some obsolete (tanks), others very high quality (fighter planes). Strategic landings in western North Africa would have the direct advantage of placing Axis forces that were hammering at the gates of Egypt in a vise.

The decision created a firestorm in Washington. The US Army was determined to fight a decisive battle in France under a grand strategic plan first formulated by Lieutenant Colonel Coady Wedemeyer; any other effort was a distraction. General George C. Marshall (Chief of Staff of the Army) and Admiral Ernest King (Commander-in-Chief, United States Fleet) were adamantly opposed to the Africa plan, feeling that it would delay landings on mainland Europe. Finally President Roosevelt ordered the operation, one of only two direct orders he gave to his service chiefs during the entire war.

In early November 1942 task forces were assigned three main objectives: one in Morocco (Casablanca) and two in Algeria (Oran and Algiers). Covert operations included making contact with senior Vichy officers to minimize the chances of resolute Vichy defense. The Western Task Force (Casablanca) under George S. Patton included one armored and two infantry divisions; the Center Task Force (Oran) an armored division, an infantry division, and a battalion of airborne infantry; and the Eastern Task Force (Algiers) with an American infantry division, a British infantry brigade, and two commando units.

On the evening of November 7 an abortive coup attempt by a French officer in Casablanca alerted the Vichy command. At Casablanca the landings took place before dawn on November 8. The surf was heavy and the night dark, so it was difficult for the sailors to locate the line of departure, and ships their assigned beaches. Soldiers drowned after their landing craft collided with ships. To add to the chaos, supplies were landed on the wrong beaches.

The Americans had hoped to meet a sympathetic French defense, but after shore batteries opened fire the supporting ships shelled shore positions. In some cases the inexperienced American infantry were pinned down by sniper fire on the beaches. The Allies did not have complete air superiority, and the landings were one of the few where an invasion was opposed by naval forces. The Vichy naval sortie resulted in the loss of a cruiser, six destroyers, and six submarines. The disabled giant battle ship *Jean Bart* was shelled into wreckage at her dock. By afternoon the landing force was better organized, and Casablanca surrendered on November 10.

At Oran American Rangers captured shore batteries, but an attempt to land at the harbor failed. Drops from aircraft flying all the way from England resulted in confused landings (out of fuel, many planes simply landed on dry lake beds), but the two airfield objectives were captured.

The Algiers landings were well-coordinated with the local resistance who for a short while isolated the senior Vichy officer in North Africa. The Resistance undertook diversionary actions, disabled shore batteries, and seized radio and telephone communication centers. As a result the landings did not encounter strong opposition and the city surrendered that evening.

ASSESSMENT: The operation proved that the Americans were indeed not ready for an invasion of Western Europe. Plans were overly complex, with multiple isolated landing beaches that were not directly supportive of each other, and unreasonable expectations for the airborne force. The American infantry was not sufficiently prepared for an amphibious assault, and naval forces inexperienced. A landing against veteran German troops would have been a disaster. The operation provided much more information about what *not* to do than the Dieppe experiment. In the greater strategic sphere, the invasion prompted the Germans to invade southern France, and to take over Tunisia in coordination with Italian troops.

The Germans were eventually forced to undertake an evacuation from Tunis, with heavy loss of equipment. It was time for the Allies to open a front in Europe. Italy was designated as the weak point of the Nazi territory. American planners opposed fighting in what Churchill called "the weak underbelly of Europe" as dissipation of effort, but in vain.

Sicily, July 9/10, 1943

The Allies decided to first take over Sicily, and a complex combined airborne/amphibious operation took place in the night of July 9/10,

1943. The landings met with little opposition due to the surprise effect and weak Italian defenses. While the Italians and Germans were getting reorganized, a large number of British, Canadian, and American troops had already landed. The primary fiasco was the airborne drop. Transport aircraft were routed above the landing ships, and after one nervous antiaircraft gunner opened fire the entire fleet blazed away at the slow, low-flying transport planes, with heavy loss of planes and lives.

Despite early successes the main Allied advance along the east coast toward the primary goal, the port of Messina, bogged down. Lieutenant General Patton seized the opportunity to push through the mountainous interior and attack eastward along the north coast, where he made good use of Allied amphibious capabilities. On the morning of August 8 a small amphibious force landed 6 miles to the rear of the German coastal defenses while an infantry division launched a frontal attack, unhinging the German defense. This tactic was so successful that Patton employed it on two more occasions.

ASSESSMENT: The initial landing in Sicily was a success in that the Allies mastered the skies and water above and around the objectives. The Italian defenders did not expect the landing since the night prior a heavy storm fell over the beaches. The advance along the north coast was more innovative than the repeated frontal attacks against river crossings and other defensive lines, as practiced by Patton's fellow generals.

Following the capture of Sicily, the Allies immediately launched Operation *Avalanche*, a landing to establish a position on the Italian peninsula. The Salerno landings went well thanks in large part to effective naval gunfire support from destroyers that moved in as close as 100 yards from the beach. The Germans fought stubbornly but the Allies were able to consolidate and expand the beachhead. Ashore the Allies eventually found themselves facing heavy resistance before strong German positions in the Italian mountains. The Allies decided to bypass the line by establishing a beachhead north of the German front.

On January 22, 1944 the Americans began landing at Anzio. There was little resistance, and a beachhead quickly established.

Inexplicably, the attackers did not exploit their early and easy success. Instead of progressing quickly inland to capture exits from the coastal plain, they established a small perimeter dominated by surrounding hills, and the offensive bogged down. When the Allies finally attempted to break out, they were faced by three German divisions in strong positions. The Allied advance could resume only after the German situation became untenable. The futile fighting in Italy would last until the German surrender in May 1945.

ASSESSMENT: At Anzio the landing phase and paratroop drops were perfectly conducted, but instead of pushing inland to open up exits from the coastal plain, the Allies paused and momentum was lost.

CHAPTER 9

~~~~~~

RETURN TO WESTERN EUROPE

*"Something in the British attitude, a faint but definitely perceptible
lack of enthusiasm for the cross-Channel concept, disturbed
Eisenhower. He had received a distinct impression that the British
were skeptical about an operation in 1942 ..."*

General Albert C. Wedemeyer, *Wedemeyer Reports!*

The Western Allies had for years been divided by disagreement over grand strategy. The Americans were champing at the bit for an invasion and decisive battle with Nazi Germany. American leaders were fearful of Soviet post-war expansionism in Europe, and besides, head-on attack in overwhelming force was the American way of war. The British had grown war-weary, and soldier-diplomat Albert Wedemeyer observed a long-standing British tendency to hang back and conduct war by proxy. They persisted in attempts to pick away at the periphery of continental Europe while the Nazis bled themselves dry on the Eastern Front. By 1944 the simple magnitude of forces had propelled the Americans into the driver's seat.

Since Dieppe the Allies had continuously improved their amphibious tactics. Now, at insistent Soviet prodding, it was time to establish a new front in Western Europe. Normandy was selected because the sector was the less heavily fortified, and because the landing beaches and nearby environment was more or less flat, unlike other beaches which were surrounded by dominating cliffs. The area behind the beaches also offered more potential for a breakout into maneuver warfare once the beachhead was established.

The Pas-de-Calais Deception, 1944

The Germans were painfully aware that the Allies were readying themselves for an invasion. But where would the blow fall? Adolf Hitler was convinced that the Allied invasion would take place at the narrowest part of the English Channel—a logical assumption.

One of the purposes of an amphibious force is to pose a threat that the enemy cannot ignore. To bolster the German misconception the Allies created a phantom amphibious force in southern England, positioned just across from the Pas-de-Calais. The deception included empty tented camps, fake radio traffic, a quarantine of "assembly areas," and even inflatable rubber tanks and trucks. Antiaircraft batteries carefully missed German observation planes. German planes flying above the western part of England were shot down with equal care. The Allies bombed all along the coast to avoid concealing the exact location of the future landings. To further cloud the issue, a diversionary force was established in Northern Ireland to let the Germans think the invasion would take place in Norway.

Who better to lead the phantom army than George Patton, who had a proven predilection for frontal assault and amphibious operations? German intelligence was convinced that such an outstanding general would not have been sidelined simply because he had slapped a junior enlisted man in the final phases of the Sicily campaign. The deception proved so effective that even after the Normandy landings Hitler declined to release German strategic reserves despite pleas from his generals, hoarding them to counter an attack that never came.

Normandy, June 6, 1944

Realistically, little needs to be said about the largest, most complex, and most studied amphibious operation in history.

Operation *Neptune* was scheduled for early June but an uncontrollable factor delayed the operation: the weather. Convoys had to cross 100 miles of sea to reach the invasion beaches. Mines and

Large and complex operations typically had a "blanket" codename, and names for components. *Neptune* was the amphibious component of *Overlord*, the overall name for the invasion of Normandy.

submarines were threats that could be dealt with, but the early June storms of the Channel were impossible to control. Fortunately for the Allies, a lull during the night of 5/6 June 1944 permitted the crossing.

Neptune was meticulously planned down to the smallest detail, and characterized by the most absolute control of the air and sea of any invasion of the war. Naval forces swept large channels free of mines, and secured the channels against attack by German submarines and torpedo boats. To avoid a repetition of the tragedy off Sicily, aircraft carrying paratroopers were specially marked, flashed special recognition signals, and where possible were routed clear of ships below.

The Luftwaffe was reduced to two fighter aircraft in position to counterattack the beachhead, while hundreds of Allied fighter-bombers and bombers swarmed over France, attacking airfields, German transportation routes, and any ground forces they could find.

Nearly 7,000 ships began crossing the Channel using different paths, transporting six divisions: Americans, British, Canadians, Polish, and small Free French units predominated, but in all, 16 countries were represented. Several hours before the waterborne troops landed, paratroopers belonging to three divisions were dropped behind enemy lines. Their missions were to disrupt (or destroy) communications behind the invasion beaches to prevent the Germans from bringing reinforcements to the beachheads, seize key objectives like bridges necessary to move inland and establish a deep and viable beachhead, and to create general confusion. The French Resistance, alerted by radio, played an important role by confusing the Germans, and harassing German units spread all across France as they tried to move toward the beachhead. Preliminary bombing began in the early hours of June 6, followed by a massive naval bombardment 90 minutes before the landing.

Five beaches were assaulted at dawn. To deal with German defenses, the British had developed specialized vehicles to open breaches in the defenses. General Percy Hobart, commanding the 79th Armored Division, and his staff developed the "funnies," including flail tanks to clear mines, Churchill heavy tanks fitted with heavy mortars in place of the main gun to destroy bunkers, tanks equipped with flamethrowers, and carpet layers to cross soft sand.

One of Hobart's funnies was the Duplex Drive tank, a standard M4 medium tank fitted with a flotation skirt and propellers. These would, in theory, provide gunfire support soon after the landing. The skirt allowed the tank to take to the water from a landing ship and reach the shore under its own power at the same time as the infantry. However, on the morning of D-Day, the surf was too heavy and many of the tanks sank or were swept along by strong offshore currents.

On four beaches the landing went according to the plan and the assault itself was a total surprise to the outnumbered defenders. On Omaha Beach, the Germans mounted a fierce resistance due to the failure of the preliminary bombardment to knock out the defenses and the absence of tanks to support the infantry.

In other sectors a junction was established a few hours after the landing with the paratroopers.

The location of the beachhead did not include large harbors: their capture might require considerable time and resources. (The nearby port of Cherbourg, considered vital, was captured on June 30 after a costly siege.) To bring enough supplies and material ashore to support the invasion the Allies built two artificial harbors codenamed Mulberries. These were massive concrete caissons towed across the Channel and assembled to provide enclosed harbors on the otherwise open beaches. To assure an uninterrupted flow of fuel, a pipeline was laid across the seabed.

ASSESSMENT: Planning was complex and meticulous, and the landings a complete success despite heavy losses. Critical German reinforcements were delayed by elaborate deceptions, cooperation with local partisans, and major airborne landings, buying the invaders precious time to expand their beachhead and

The logistics of any major amphibious landing are nightmarish, as illustrated by the Normandy landings. The task might be likened to relocating an entire city of 100,000 inhabitants or more, complete with all its infrastructure. (Library of Congress)

quickly transition from an amphibious assault to a large landmass offensive.

The Allied offensive in Italy was proving a major disappointment. To speed their drive to Germany, it was decided to open a new front in southern Europe, Operation *Dragoon*. The beaches of southeastern France were selected, since the large natural corridor formed by the Rhône Valley would allow a pincer attack on German units trapped in France.

On June 15 some 600 ships approached the Provence coast. The usual plan of attack called for paratroopers to drop a few miles behind the beaches to cut access to German reinforcements. Commandos were landed east and west of the objective to neutralize coastal batteries that could have threatened the operation.

The landing itself began after an intense preparatory fire from bombers and naval artillery. The beaches were poorly defended and

American actor and US Navy Lieutenant Commander Douglas Fairbanks Jr. created and commanded the Beach Jumpers, a special Navy unit that staged fake landings to deceive the Germans in the Mediterranean Theater. Their greatest exploit was in southern France in support of *Dragoon*.

Germans quickly overwhelmed. Forces were dispatched to secure Marseille and Toulon for their deep-water harbors.

The Scheldt, October 2–November 8, 1944

The requirement for amphibious operations did not end in France. The logistical requirements of the Allied armies necessitated the capture of large ports, and Antwerp in Belgium was a prime objective. The port sits some 40 miles up the winding Scheldt Estuary that was dominated by German shore positions. The Germans flooded much of the surrounding *polders* (drained land), creating a nightmarish gigantic marsh. The ensuing campaign was a brutal, muddy slog under heavy fire, with crossings of canals and channels effected with the aid of LVTs. The Canadian 9th Brigade mounted in British LVTs conducted a surprise shore-to-shore landing (part of Operation *Switchback*), that moved down the river, and gained a foothold on the southern shore of the estuary, and bypassing a large inlet that blocked the advance. British and Canadian troops attacked westward along the south shore of the river. On October 24 British troops crossed the Scheldt onto South Beveland (Operation *Vitality*). On November 1 the Allies staged a final major shore-to-shore landing (Operation *Infatuate*) with troops ferried across from the south bank onto Walcheren Island in twenty British Landing Craft, Assaults. The attack was directly into strong German defenses for the port of Vlissingen (Flushing to the Allies) while other units attacked across a narrow causeway from North Beveland to the east. On November 8, 1944 about 40,000 Germans remaining on Walcheren surrendered. By the end of the month supplies were flowing through Antwerp.

CHAPTER 10

~~~~~~

THE COLD WAR

"The amphibious landing of US Marines on September 1950 at Inchon, on the west coast of Korea, was one of the most audacious and spectacularly successful amphibious landings in all naval history."

Bernard Brodie, *A Guide to Naval Strategy*

Many historians consider the amphibious assault the most important factor in winning the war against the Axis powers, but in the immediate aftermath of World War II the doctrine was again declared dead. The theory was that nuclear weapons rendered the necessary concentration of naval vessels vulnerable. As the US Marine Cops searched for a new role in a collapsing national military establishment, they were confronted by a new and unrealistic theory. The US Army's strategic doctrine was that nuclear bombers could simply bomb an enemy into submission, and troops transported by air (the future Strategic Army Corps or STRAC) could be sent in to pacify the rubble. In retrospect it was amazingly naïve, as little had been learned about the staying power of airborne forces.

Inter-service rivalries were further complicated by efforts to transfer all aviation assets to the new Air Force, expeditionary missions to the Army, and reduce the Corps back to a naval security force—if not to eliminate it altogether. Again the Navy, foreseeing the need for force projection into newly volatile but relatively remote regions like the Middle East, was the Marine Corps' savior. Still, the bureaucratic battles dragged on through the late 1940s, with relentless budget cuts. Efforts to gut the Corps continued into 1950, but America would soon face a war in a distant land with only a shadow remaining of its amphibious capabilities.

The Marine Corps slowly forged ahead in the development of a new generation of amphibious assault vehicles, but the next war would be fought with upgraded versions of World War II equipment. Foremost among them were upgraded LVT-3 amphibious tractors fitted with overhead armor to provide some protection against airbursts and nuclear radiation. The cannon-armed LVT(A)-5 was similarly modernized to serve as an ersatz amphibious tank.

In the geopolitical wilderness that followed the collapse of European colonialism, old adversaries simply resumed their local feuds. Some were local in nature, others were efforts to overthrow resurgent colonial rule, as in the Dutch East Indies. When Communist-fomented civil wars in places like Greece failed, attempts by increasingly active Communist insurgencies to subvert colonial or pro-Western governments in "wars of national liberation" became the norm. Most were of a nature that left little scope for orthodox military operations.

The Chinese Civil War, 1927–1950

By far the most geopolitically important conflict was the Chinese Civil War between the Communists and nationalist Kuomintang forces. Chinese territory included many nearby islands, the largest being Hainan and Formosa (Taiwan). As the Communist forces gained the upper hand, nationalist forces were driven onto the islands.

Initial Communist attempts at amphibious operations against smaller islands were disasters. In late October of 1949 a Communist landing on Kinmen resulted in the annihilation of the landing force within two days. A landing on Dengbu was a lesser disaster, though the island was later surrendered when it was rendered untenable by increasing Communist air superiority.

The initial assault on Hainan by Communist forces in March 1950 miscarried when a hastily organized fleet of junks carrying about 800 men lost its way and landed at the most strongly defended point. It was slaughtered to a man, but when the defenders rushed forces to this landing site the main Communist force came ashore elsewhere against minimal opposition.

Over the following days, flotillas of small craft transported additional Communist forces to the island. The Kuomintang defenders botched their greatest opportunity to disrupt the landings when a fleet led by their single destroyer engaged one flotilla in a comic-opera sea battle. The destroyer flagship raced into point-blank range, thinking the small boats were unarmed. Instead the small craft opened fire with light artillery pieces; the destroyer could not depress its guns to fire back, and beat an ignominious retreat. Other smaller craft engaged the ramshackle Communist fleet, but their armor-piercing ammunition simply passed through the light craft. The Communists continued to pour in forces in penny-packets, and by April overwhelmed the defenders by sheer numbers.

ASSESSMENT: The Communists learned from early mistakes, and Hainan is the only modern capture of a major objective by such an ad-hoc amphibious force, a kind of "Dunkirk in reverse." Communist goals were increasingly directed toward more conventional land warfare with its neighbors like India, intervention in Korea, and internal purges. China would not witness a rebirth of interest in an amphibious capability for another half-century.

The Korean War, 1950–1953

The protracted but undeclared war of 1950–1953 witnessed two of the most successful amphibious operations in history, though only one is widely acclaimed. When the North Korean People's Army (NKPA) swept south in a surprise offensive in the summer of 1950, they brushed aside the underequipped Republic of Korea (ROK) Army and contingents of the US Army, grown soft from occupation duty in Japan. Despite heroic and often self-sacrificial resistance, the Americans and the ROK found themselves penned into a small beachhead around the port of Pusan.

The brilliant but egotistical General Douglas MacArthur had been one of the more innovative practitioners of amphibious warfare in World War II, and conceived a bold strategic stroke. NKPA successes had left them overextended, with almost all forces deployed around Pusan. Their weakness was that their long road and rail supply lines passed through a narrow zone in western Korea, near the port of Inchon. Severing the supply lines would lead to a rapid collapse of the forces surrounding Pusan, and recapture the politically important South Korean capital, Seoul.

The only problem was that MacArthur's chosen invasion site, the port of Inchon, was one of the worst places in the world to stage an amphibious assault. In 1950 (more recent construction has radically changed the local geography) Inchon lay far up a narrow channel dominated by surrounding terrain. Particularly troublesome were artillery positions on the island of Wolmi-do that would threaten the main landing sites from behind. The city was bounded by marshland, and the main landing force would have to come over a high stone seawall directly into the city. The plan combined the two worst military scenarios: amphibious assault and urban combat. Worst of all, the port was subject to extreme tidal variations that left the ship channel impassable at low tide. Any landing force would have to go ashore at high tide, but would find itself isolated until the next high tide. To further complicate matters, the element of surprise would be lost, the operation betrayed by necessary naval minesweeping and bombardments.

A considerable organizational struggle ensued, but MacArthur prevailed by force of personality and reputation. The US Army, fixated on a potential land war against the Soviets in Europe, had given up most of its hard-won amphibious expertise. The US Marine Corps had been hollowed out to a shell of its 1945 strength, and the 1st Marine Division was hastily reconstructed from whatever troops were available. Advisors hastily retrained the Army's 7th Infantry Division in amphibious warfare. A successful disinformation operation convinced the NKPA that the landings would be at Gunsan, far to the south and a more orthodox site.

MacArthur's risky Inchon operation depended upon attacking directly into the port itself. These heavily-burdened Marines in an LCVP are equipped with crude scaling ladders, with steel hooks on the upper ends, to surmount the stone seawall. (Marine Corps History Division)

At 0630 hours on September 15 Operation *Chromite* began when a Marine battalion landing team supported by tanks landed on Wolmi-do and quickly secured the island. As the tide receded, the Marines set up hasty defenses. At the next high tide, at 1730 hours, the main landing forces attacked the seawall, and landed on mud beaches to the south. In anticipation of the next low tide LSTs (Landing Ships, Tank), some loaded with supplies and others equipped as hospitals, were deliberately left stranded on the mudflats.

Soldiers and Marines poured ashore, and the tanks and infantry on Wolmi-do crossed the causeway that connected the island to the city. The successful invasion, and a coordinated offensive from Pusan, led to a complete collapse of the NKPA.

Despite ominous rumblings from North Korea's patron, China, MacArthur decided to sweep north to the Manchurian border and unify the Koreas. The advance was so rapid that amphibious forces reembarked from Inchon for a landing on the east coast but were beaten to the landing sites by advancing land forces.

The LARC-V (five) amphibious truck is a huge improvement over the World War II era DUKW. The low cargo bed allows easier loading, and the boat-shaped hull is more stable in surf. (National Archives)

United Nations forces in northeastern Korea pushed almost to the Yalu River border, but in late November the Chinese struck. Their plan was to crush the 1st Marine Division and the attached 32nd Infantry Regiment and seize the main port at Hungnam: all other UN forces would be trapped and destroyed. An epic fighting retreat not only extricated the American force, but bought time for the US Army's 3rd Division to organize a defense of the port.

Operation *Christmas Cargo* was a largely unrecognized masterpiece, bringing off nearly 100,000 troops and all their equipment without further loss. Another 100,000 Korean civilians were evacuated, and one overloaded ship, the USS *Meredith Victory*, brought off 14,000 civilians, the largest shipboard rescue in history.

ASSESSMENT: The Inchon landing is considered the most brilliant amphibious operation in history, both for the way in which nearly insuperable obstacles were overcome, and for its tactical and strategic effects. The evacuation of Hungnam was an event that no one could have planned for, but the hard-won expertise of the US Navy led to complete success instead of a catastrophe.

A new generation of amphibious assault tractor, the LVTP-5, entered service in 1956. With a fully enclosed hull and capacity of up to 40 troops, it was far more capable than the older LVTs. A replacement for the aging DUKW was the Lighter, Amphibious

Many "amphibious" vehicles are designed for river crossings, with low survivability in surf. The Soviet BTR-50 personnel carrier was developed from the PT-76 light tank, with similarly limited amphibious capability. This BTR-50PK, captured by the Israelis, has a thin armored roof to provide some protection for the passengers. (Defense Intelligence Agency)

Resupply, Cargo, 5 ton (LARC-V). Still in use in modernized form, it is a truck with a boat-shaped hull, low sides for better cargo handling, and four oversized wheels.

The Soviet Union in particular sought to improve its amphibious capabilities with the 1951 introduction of the PT-76 light tank and derivative BTR-50 personnel carrier. Although these vehicles introduced innovative features like water-jet propulsion, they were designed for river crossings, with little chance of survival in surf. In true amphibious landings they had to be deposited in very shallow water by landing craft.

Suez, October–November 1956

Egyptian strongman Gamal Abdel Nasser forcibly seized control of the Suez Canal on July 30, 1956, much to the concern of the British and French governments. The two secretly endorsed an Israeli invasion of the Sinai Peninsula, lodging a *pro forma* "ultimatum" for a ceasefire that was conveniently ignored by Israel. The continuance of the fighting provided a pretext for British and French intervention.

Beginning on October 29 the Israelis seized key objectives with airborne assaults, but Egyptian forces sank ships in the Canal, blocking it. On October 31 the Anglo-French Operation *Musketeer* commenced with a bombing campaign against Egyptian targets.

French General André Beaufre, over the objections of his more timid ally, ordered airborne forces to seize positions along the Canal on November 5, without the prospect of immediate support from amphibious forces. On the morning of November 6 the Royal Marines of No. 40 and No. 42 Commandos landed at Port Said, supported by LVTs and Centurion tanks. That afternoon parachutists of 1er Régiment Étranger de Parachutistes, supported by light tanks, landed near Port Fouad, while No. 45 Commando landed by helicopter.

Meanwhile the Americans and Soviets grew increasingly wary of the fighting that might drag them into an armed confrontation, and rushed through a United Nations mandate for a ceasefire. Although fighting ceased, the Suez Canal would remain closed to international shipping for four more months.

ASSESSMENT: The results of the aborted operation were geopolitical, and profound. The failure was a political humiliation for France and Britain: both lost regional influence and bases. Nasser ruthlessly cemented his power. Israel emerged in a better strategic position, having established itself as a major regional land warfare power. Despite its role in ending the fighting, American regional influence declined, paving the way for greater Soviet influence. Like all too many combined amphibious/airborne operations it was chaotic with much improvisation and a confused command structure. The insertion of Royal Marines by helicopter at Port Said provided an early vision of things to come.

The Suez incident indirectly plunged Lebanon into civil war between Muslims and Maronite Christians. In July 1958 two battalions of American Marines seized the Beirut harbor and airport, with rapid reinforcement by airlifted Army troops. The Marines were

A short-lived emphasis on "lightness" resulted in the substitution of light artillery and armor in American amphibious forces. This M50 Ontos tank destroyer is landing in Lebanon in 1958; the passengers are Lebanese Army officers. (Marine Corps History Division)

bedeviled by the usual logistics problems, including no main gun ammunition for their tanks. The landing force was able to quickly restore the control of the elected government and withdraw.

The early 1960s were a period of upheaval in basic assumptions that governed the future of amphibious warfare. The Western powers faced the possibility of an overwhelming Soviet conventional attack anywhere around the periphery of their Eurasian empire. Any reaction would be hampered by external lines of communication and Soviet numerical superiority. One answer seemed to be the Strategic Army Corps of airborne and light infantry. The historically demonstrable problem was that light forces lacked staying power.

The obvious solution was the stationing of amphibious reaction forces near where allied forces might face a direct land attack. As the dominant power in the alliance most under threat, the North Atlantic Treaty Organization (NATO), the United States would bear the burden of defending a perimeter that reached from northern Norway to the Persian Gulf. The mission was given to the US Marine Corps, who stationed Battalion Landing Teams (later called Marine Expeditionary Units) aboard ship. Each consisted of an infantry battalion with detachments of tanks, artillery, logistic support, and supported by naval aviation.

A review board carried the concept a bit too far by advocating conversion of the Marine Corps into "light" divisions, with the heaviest armor being the thinly armored air-portable Ontos tank destroyer, and artillery equipped with Howtars, 106mm mortars mounted on the old 75mm pack howitzer frame. Heavier weapons would be vested at the multidivision amphibious corps level.

In April 1965 civil war erupted in the Dominican Republic, and "loyalists" supporting the acting president clashed with the "constitutionalists," who had been unwise enough to incorporate leftists. Fearful of Communist influence, the United States intervened unilaterally, with Organization of American States troops to follow. On April 30 amphibious and airborne troops landed, and by the end of the day a ceasefire had been negotiated. Sporadic fighting continued, but with government power restored the last foreign troops left on September 3. The operation was notable for the first significant use of helicopters in an American amphibious operation.

The Indochina Experience, 1946–1975

The end of the Korean War ushered in a new era of "wars of national liberation," primarily Communist guerilla struggles against Western-backed democracies or dictatorships. The defining experience was the decades-long struggle in Indochina. When the French sought to reestablish colonial dominance in the late 1940s, they found themselves deploying conventional forces in a countryside with limited roads. Southern Vietnam was always seen as a secondary theater to the Hanoi region, but there numerous waterways provided the primary means of transport. The French were quick to organize *Divisions navales d'assaut*, or *Dinassaut* riverine units with American landing craft, as well as amphibious vehicles like the DUKW truck, the M29 Weasel, as well as LVTs (some with awkwardly mounted 40mm antiaircraft guns), LVT(A)1s, and 4s as personnel carriers.

Most amphibious operations were for reconnaissance but on March 13, 1954 an amphibious assault on the coastal city of Qui Nhon was conducted well behind Viet Minh lines. The landing site was poorly defended and French troops quickly entered the city to clear it of isolated snipers. A larger ground force attacked from the south to link up with the beachhead. Such a minor operation, no matter how successful, was unable to turn the tide of the conflict. The French were forced to abandon Indochina the next year.

When the Americans entered the conflict in early 1965 the first ground troops were Marines of the 9th Marine Expeditionary Brigade, chosen because the Marines were self-sustaining, with their own organic logistical and support services. The initial entry was almost a parody of an amphibious operation: the Marines splashed ashore, greeted by vendors and young women distributing garlands of flowers.

The Marines were at first used as ordinary infantry, providing base security, but leaders were eager to test their new "triphibious" assault doctrine that combined amphibious operations with closely integrated airmobile operations. Intelligence indicated that the Communist Viet Cong (VC) were assembling for an attack on the logistics base at Chu-Lai, and organized a complex operation, *Starlite*, to preempt the enemy offensive. Some units moved by land mounted in LVTs to establish blocking positions, infantry and tanks assaulted nearby beaches, and other infantry landed inland by helicopter.

Heliborne and amphibious units pushed the VC back against the sea, and trapped other large units in an inland village complex. More heliborne infantry was inadvertently landed almost atop a VC fortified village, with bloody and confused fighting. Sporadic fighting continued for five days as infantry rooted out hidden enemy survivors, but all too many of the enemy had slipped away to fight another day.

ASSESSMENT: Although considered by many to be the most successful amphibious operation of the war, the operation was marred by inexperience, poor coordination, and poor communications. *Starlite* set the pattern for numerous other named seaborne raids, mounted to keep the enemy off balance, but the amphibious war around the eastern ocean perimeter was fairly insignificant in the bigger struggle.

The Navy–Marine Corps team had created Special Landing Forces (SLF), built around a rifle battalion and its supporting assets, to support Pacific Fleet operations, and two such forces (SLF-A and SLF-B) were deployed off Vietnam. The function of the SLF resurrected the command issue that had long bedeviled amphibious operations: exactly who was in charge at what phase of the operation? The major issue was that while still aboard ship, the 7th Fleet structure should logically control troops. Once the initial landing phase ended, tactical control should pass to the landing force commander.

The complication in Vietnam was that all forces ashore were under control of the Army's Military Assistance Command, Vietnam (MACV), and its subordinate III Marine Amphibious Force. Thus the handoff was not to a landing force commander, but to an entirely different command structure. Problems were exacerbated by the technicality that the naval force commander reported not to MACV but to 7th Fleet. All too often naval commanders simply refused to declare the landing phase completed, thereby creating considerable animosity with army counterparts.

The US Navy organized riverine forces for a variety of tasks, using both heavily modified landing craft and specially built light river craft. The first major riverine offensive was Operation *Jackstay*, in late March and early April of 1966, which highlighted the complexity of joint operations.

The Rung Sat Special Zone was a complex of nearly impenetrable swamps and marshes that dominated the shipping channel between Saigon and the sea. Long the lair of pirates, smugglers, and common criminals, the region now harbored major VC forces. A complex combination of American and South Vietnamese forces, *Jackstay* included helicopter assaults from both land bases and ships, river patrols that blocked enemy operations and inserted troops, and infantry assaults from the surrounding countryside.

Back to the roots of amphibious warfare. These American Marine Corps advisors are patrolling with South Vietnamese Popular Forces militia in crude canoes. (Marine Corps History Division)

The Vietnam experience led to the 1972 introduction of the **LVTP-7** (later Amphibian Assault Vehicle, or AAV). With improved water-jet propulsion, durable suspension, and the ability to operate briefly with the engine deck submerged, it was and remains the most capable amphibious vehicle in history.

An additional innovation that would indirectly affect the future of amphibious warfare was the introduction of "**pull logistics**." The use of computers to track actual consumption of supplies rather than using past experience, combined with more efficient cargo handling, would result in far more efficient operational logistics, always crucial with limited transport capacity.

The late Vietnam-era LVTP-7 was redesigned and re-designated the Assault Amphibian Vehicle shown here. It remains the most capable and versatile amphibious troop carrier ever deployed, and is used by numerous countries. Later models have a larger turret with an additional automatic 40mm grenade launcher, and additional armor to increase survivability in land combat. (National Archives)

The operation succeeded in disrupting VC operations in the region for a longer period that usual. But in the end the Americans and South Vietnamese suffered from the same problem as the French: there was never enough manpower to occupy and control huge areas of countryside.

Eventually the growing intensity of the land fighting required the commitment of the Marine Corps' amphibious specialists as ordinary infantry. The importance of amphibious operations withered, and expertise along with it. The protracted war had inflicted damage to America's amphibious warfare capabilities that would take a decade to heal.

Regional Conflicts, 1960s–1990s

The period saw many localized conflicts not connected to the greater Cold War. The Nigerian Civil War, or Biafran War, was triggered by the July 1967 secession of part of oil-rich Nigeria. Britain in particular had major investments and sided with the central government, while France supported secessionist Biafra. The United States and the Soviet Union stood aloof.

As government forces pushed the Biafrans southward they became increasingly dependent upon their only remaining port, Calabar. Operation *Tiger Claw* was an October 17–19 assault on the port by Nigerian Marines. The capture severed Biafra's connections to the outside world, and the war degenerated into years of famine and genocide.

In the long struggle in Northern Ireland Britain launched Operation *Motorman*, its biggest, but virtually unknown, amphibious operation since the Suez Crisis. The cities of Belfast and Derry had grown increasingly divided and rebellious, with the establishment of "no go" zones controlled by local Protestant or Irish Republican Army militias. On July 31, 1972 about 4,000 troops, supported by engineer tanks put ashore from the LPD HMS *Fearless*, swept through Derry and within hours demolished barricades that had divided the city into warring sectors.

Cyprus, 1974

While the attention of the world was fixed upon major power proxy struggles, the Turkish military pulled off one of the most audacious and strategically successful amphibious operations in history. Resentment and militia clashes had long marked the mainly urban Turkish minority attitude toward the mainly rural Greek majority on Cyprus. The Turks had sent out invasion fleets on previous occasions, only to be turned back by diplomatic negotiations. On July 20 a Greek-sponsored coup deposed the Cypriot president, planning to annex the island. On July 20 another Turkish fleet did not turn back, but landed unopposed at the coastal town of Kyrenia, north of the capital, Nicosia. A Turkish command and control group was inserted by air into the Nicosia airport to coordinate forces. Parachutists landed at the airport, and troops in helicopters secured sites on the road connecting the cities. The invasion was supported by, but not coordinated with, uprisings by Turkish civilians. Most were suppressed, but Turkish militia seized and held a medieval fortress that dominated the road until reinforced by parachutists.

The ethnic Greek National Guard was too disorganized to offer significant resistance, and Greek ships carrying supplies and reinforcements were repulsed by Turkish ships. By afternoon some 6,000 Turkish troops and 60 tanks were ashore, and helicopters were airlifting reinforcements and light vehicles into the airport. By nightfall the Turks controlled the road.

ASSESSMENT: The more numerous Greek defenders had grown complacent and disorganized, unable to offer any significant reaction to an overt daylight invasion. The invasion was an example of excellent cooperation among amphibious, airborne, and heliborne assault troops, supported by a "fifth column" of local militias and civilian sympathizers. The final resolution was a UN-brokered ceasefire and forced relocations into Greek and Turkish zones that still divide the island.

The Failed Iran Rescue Mission, April 1980

On November 4, 1979 Iranian revolutionaries overran the US embassy in Tehran and took captive about 90 people including 66 Americans. Negotiations failed to win their release, and on April 24, 1980 the US undertook a complex and poorly organized rescue mission.

Eight heavy-lift Navy helicopters would rendezvous at a remote desert base with Air Force C-130 aircraft carrying necessary fuel and supplies. The entire force would hide in the desert. On the second night special operations forces would raid the embassy where the hostages were held, and move them to a nearby helicopter landing zone. From there the helicopters would transport them to a nearby Iranian airbase to be captured by Army Rangers, where they would be loaded aboard Air Force transport planes.

The entire plan was overly complex. When equipment failures, dust storms, and delays threw off time schedules and fuel consumption calculations, refueling efforts at the remote desert site resulted in the collision of a helicopter and one of the refueling planes. The mission was fatally off-track, and was aborted.

ASSESSMENT: The entire plan was overly complex, and required everything to go according to plan. It required coordination among Central Intelligence Agency, Army, Navy, Air Force, and Marine Corps personnel who had not worked or trained together and were not familiar with each other's methods and capabilities. It was probably doomed from the start.

The Falklands War, April–June 1982

During the Cold War era Britain let its amphibious capabilities atrophy. In the meantime many strictly regional powers grew in power. Argentina had long laid claim to the British-administered Falkland Islands (Islas Malvinas) in the southern Atlantic, and domestic pressures led them to attempt a seizure of the islands.

Argentina had a small but significant amphibious warfare capability. On the night of April 1/2 Argentine naval commandos landed covertly from the destroyer *Santisima Trinidad* in an attempt to surprise the Royal Marine garrison. The British Marines had instead withdrawn to defend Government House.

The main landing was made using 20 American-built LVTP-7 amphibian tractors and two large landing craft, and the tractors led a road march toward Port Stanley. The Argentines were under orders to avoid inflicting casualties in this strange war, but not so the Royal Marines, who destroyed at least two LVTs with antitank rockets. The last-ditch defenders at Government House were eventually forced to surrender under the threat of superior Argentine firepower.

By April 5 the British dispatched a naval task force to regain control of the waters around the Falklands, but any attack would have to be staged from Ascension Island, over 4,500 miles away. The British cobbled together a fleet that included 62 civilian vessels, including the liners SS *Canberra* and SS *Queen Elizabeth II* as troop transports. A major issue would be to establish air superiority over the more numerous Argentine air force; long-range bombing raids from Ascension Island caused the Argentines to evacuate aircraft from the islands.

The British first recaptured South Georgia, east of the Falklands, with minimal resistance. The struggle for naval superiority was more costly, with the Argentines losing a cruiser and the British a destroyer.

In the night of May 21/22 the British launched a counterinvasion, landing from Royal Navy transports, river barges, and civilian vessels like the ferry *Norland*. Argentine aerial attacks took a heavy toll of both naval and civilian vessels, though losses would have been heavier but for the Argentine tactic of releasing drag-retarded bombs from too low an altitude.

The landing force moved quickly overland to capture the Argentine base at Goose Green. Subsequent landing operations were slow and confused, primarily as the result of high-level orders not to risk the Landing Platform, Dock assault ship HMS *Intrepid* and the Landing Ship, Logistics HMS *Sir Tristam* close to land. The slow movement of landing craft from far out at sea exposed them to air attack, with heavy loss of life.

The British were eventually able to pour sufficient men ashore to recapture the main town of Port Stanley, and establish airbases to fend off further Argentine attacks.

ASSESSMENT: The brief Falklands War demonstrated that overcoming logistical difficulties was a lesson to be relearned. New weapons systems like antiship missiles that caused considerable havoc among the British fleet reinforced the lesson that absolute air superiority was necessary to protect vulnerable ships sitting stationary offshore. Geopolitically the war bolstered the strength of the Conservative Party in British politics, and led to loss of the military's long-standing grip on domestic politics in Argentina.

The British experience in the Falklands was a major wakeup call for the US military. In the aftermath of Vietnam the US Marine Corps had reassessed its amphibious mission, leading to another major revision of amphibious doctrine. Reaction time required to form and deploy heavy forces had always been too slow, and the solution was the Maritime Prepositioning Ship concept. Sufficient heavy equipment, fuel, ammunition, and other stores to equip a Marine division would be kept aboard ships stationed in the major oceans. In time of need troops could be airlifted in to mate up with these weapons and stores. Instituted in 1985–1986,

The Landing Craft, Air Cushion or LCAC allows ships to remain safely out at sea but still deliver heavy equipment like this M1A1 tank directly onto the beach at high speed. (National Archives)

this doctrinal innovation would face its first real-life test within five years.

In the late 1980s the Soviet Union and China began to develop small "blue water" navies for regional force projection, with concomitant amphibious capabilities. The Soviets in particular began the deployment of true amphibious transport ships, primarily modern landing ships capable of depositing tanks and heavy vehicles directly onto the beach. Another innovation that appeared nearly simultaneously in the US and USSR was the Air-Cushioned Landing Craft (LCAC). With inflatable pontoons for flotation, skirts that allow the powerful engines to generate a layer of air on which the vessel rides, and propeller or jet engines for forward propulsion, the LCAC can ride swiftly atop the water, then directly up onto a sloping beach to deposit its cargo. American LCACs are designed to operate from larger landing ships, and carry vehicles including 70-ton M1-series tanks. Some Soviet classes were significantly larger, but were designed to operate in waters like the Black Sea or Baltic.

The Sri Lankan Civil War, July 1983–May 2009

The war fought by the "Tamil Tiger" secessionists was marked by both guerrilla fighting and conventional warfare. The Tigers controlled much of northern and eastern Sri Lanka, with scattered and isolated enclaves under government control. In November 1990 the government position near the major rebel supply port of Mullaitivu in northeastern Sri Lanka was besieged, but was relieved and reinforced by a hasty amphibious landing, Operation *Sea Breeze*.

In July 1991 a major government position at Elephant Pass, a passageway through coastal sand dunes that controlled the land approaches to the northernmost tip of Sri Lanka, was besieged by the Tigers. With no secure land route to the base, the Sri Lankan military hastily organized Operation *Balavegaya*, a force of about 10,000 troops transported aboard a motley fleet of landing craft, gunboats, and other small vessels.

The first attempt at a landing in the early afternoon of July 15 was driven off, but another landing at 1800 hours was supported by a massive naval bombardment. The landing force, including armored cars, quickly bogged down in brutal fighting; it took 18 days for the landing force to fight its way seven miles to effect a relief of the base.

American entanglement in the Middle East proper had grown inexorably, and in 1983 the US Marines returned to Beirut, now wrecked by years of civil war among religious factions, and cross-border attacks by Palestinian exiles that regularly provoked overwhelmingly destructive Israeli armed incursions. The landings were again unopposed and uneventful, followed by occupation of key locations in Beirut. Growing violence by Iranian–backed rebels resulted in the disastrous October 23 suicide truck-bomb attacks on the Marine barracks at the airport and French airborne troop positions in the city.

Loss of Expertise—Grenada, October 1983

A leftist government seized power in Grenada soon after its independence from Britain in 1974, and over the course of five years the internal power struggles became increasingly violent, with increasing Cuban influence. In October 1983 the national leader and many government officials were murdered in a violent military coup. Six days later on October 25 a coalition, dominated by the United States, launched an amphibious and airborne assault on the island. Army Rangers undertook an airborne assault to establish an airhead at the main southern airfield, while the Marines launched an amphibious assault at the northern end of the island. With heavier equipment like tanks and amphibious tractors for transport, the landing force was able to sweep down the coastal roads while more lightly equipped airborne forces were penned in. Within three days organized resistance had ceased, although minor fighting continued on outlying islands.

ASSESSMENT: Although outrageously successful, the invasion was marred by inadequate intelligence and reconnaissance, poor communication and coordination among the Army, Navy, and Marine Corps, and various special operations components of the invasion force; deadly friendly fire incidents resulted from the poor intelligence. Once again logistics were an issue, with some units landed without adequate ammunition. Even given the hasty organization, American forces were still floundering with combined arms and joint airborne–amphibious cooperation.

With the Cold War drawing to a close as the Soviet Union teetered toward collapse, the United States was emerging as the single greatest global power. Neither the Soviets nor Chinese had ever developed a true global reach. The United States was fortunate in that its next significant force-projection operation, the December 1989 invasion of Panama, could be launched from existing bases within that country. Amphibious operations remained the primary method of conventional force projection, but clearly the United States military had lost much of its expertise in the decades-long struggle to counter Communist insurgencies. Failure of the Iran rescue mission, the Beirut suicide bombings, and the floundering but ultimately successful Grenada invasion led to considerable soul-searching in the American military. Clearly better planning, improved inter-service cooperation, and better intelligence were all necessary.

CHAPTER 11

THE POST-COLD WAR ERA AND THE MODERN MIDDLE EAST

"The Middle East is not part of the world that plays by Las Vegas rules: what happens in the Middle East is not going to stay in the Middle East."

General David Petraeus

The end of the Cold War resulted more in a diffusion of effort than a peace. Regional foes, cut loose from the control of major power patrons, resumed old grudges. None would be bloodier than that between the religious/nationalist forces of Iran and the forces under the dictator Saddam Hussein in Iraq. The seeds of the war dated back to the Cold War when the United States viewed Saddam as a useful counter to the growing power of revolutionary Iran.

The Iraqi invasion of Iran in September 1980 triggered a savage eight-year war. The nominal cause of the conflict was over the Shatt-al-Arab waterway that formed the boundary between the two, but most fighting was conventional warfare farther inland. Deadlocked there, the Iranians decided to conduct offensives through the marshes of the lower Tigris–Euphrates river valley. The Iranians used troops mounted in speedboats and helicopters to establish beachheads on dryer ground within the marshes, then constructed causeways to move in more conventional forces. The battle of the Marshes took advantage of the Iranian superiority in manpower to counter Iraqi superiority in airpower, armor, and artillery.

The climactic battle took place over February and March 1984 when Iran seized a foothold on Majnoon Island. Taking advantage of hideous casualties inflicted by mustard gas and unconventional weapons like high-powered electrical cables immersed in the water to electrocute Iranian infantry, the Iraqis were able to stall and then drive back the Iranians.

In February 16 the Iranians launched an amphibious attack to capture the al-Faw Peninsula under cover of heavy rains that neutralized Iraqi air superiority. Iraqi counterattacks were ineffective and strategically the closure of the Shatt al-Arab created uproar in the Arab states for which Iraq was acting as a proxy.

When the war sputtered to its end, Saddam Hussein was angered by what he saw as the failure of other Arab states to help defray the catastrophic costs of the Iran war. A territorial dispute with Kuwait then ensued. When Iraq invaded Kuwait, a coalition of forces was organized to drive the Iraqis out of Kuwait. A fundamental part of the plan was to deceive the Iraqis with the threat of an amphibious assault to pin down forces that might otherwise resist a land offensive. The US Marine Corps could not in actuality deploy enough forces for a major amphibious assault because of a shortage of suitable Navy vessels, and many of those available were not suited to amphibious assault operations. Additional problems were the heavy commitment of limited resources to the land offensive, including intelligence, engineering, and other assets. It was decided to utilize the amphibious force as a strategic distraction.

The threat of an amphibious assault could not be discounted by the Iraqis, who positioned at least six infantry divisions, a mechanized division, and other units to defend the Kuwaiti and Iraqi coastline against two brigades of American Marines. Iraqi engineering assets and resources like mines were diverted from the land defenses. The mere presence of the amphibious force offshore kept these forces pinned in place when the main land assault began.

In the end the only actual amphibious attacks were small raids to seize offshore oil platforms, and the neutralization of Iraqi radar positions that aided in opening air corridors for Coalition aircraft in the final assault.

ASSESSMENT: The British strategic theoretician Sir B. H. Lidell Hart had long ago noted that the distraction provided by an amphibious threat could be grossly out of proportion to the small size of the assault force, since sea mobility allows it to threaten a very large area. The very presence of the amphibious force looming offshore pinned down between 16 and 23 percent of total Iraqi resources.

Humanitarian functions—famine and disaster relief, restoration of civil law—had been part of amphibious operations since the early 20th century, primarily because amphibious forces are self-sustaining. Operation *Restore Hope* in Somalia in 1991 blurred the distinction between combat and humanitarian missions. With no central government the country was dominated by clan warfare, with famine as a weapon.

On December 9, 1992 American Marines conducted an unopposed landing on the airport and port of Mogadishu using rubber boats, amphibious tractors, and helicopters. The amphibious force with its armored vehicles and emphasis on foot patrols (which the locals respected as warrior-like) within the city was soon replaced by light infantry with emphasis on helicopter mobility (which the locals despised). The replacement of the heavy landing force with light infantry and Pakistani light armor was cited by some as a contributing factor to a disastrous failed raid that led to the eventual UN withdrawal from the country.

In the aftermath of the September 11, 2001 terrorist attacks the initial Coalition response was for Special Operations units to attack terrorist bases in Afghanistan in coordination with local fighters of the Afghan Northern Alliance. In the second phase permanent bases needed to be established. The 15th Marine Expeditionary Unit (MEU) was diverted from a humanitarian mission to the Pakistani coast. On November 25 elements of the 15th MEU were brought in by CH-53E heavy-lift helicopters some 400 miles from the sea to establish the first base, Camp Rhino, near Kandahar. This base, and the next objective, the Kandahar airport, provided the first secure airheads for larger forces to follow by airlift.

Although it was primarily a land offensive, amphibious forces would play a significantly greater role in the second war with Iraq

Modern military equipment can be quite eclectic. These Egyptian marines have Russian small arms and BTR-50 personnel carriers, but the helicopters are American-made. (National Archives)

in March, 2003. American Marines spearheaded an attack up the Tigris–Euphrates valley. Rapid capture of the al-Faw Peninsula was considered essential to prevent another ecological disaster if the Iraqis wrecked petroleum production facilities, to eliminate Iraqi armored units based there that might threaten the rear of the main Coalition attack, and to open a waterway to bring in humanitarian supplies after the fighting ceased.

The operation was conducted by 3 Commando Brigade of the Royal Marines, reinforced by the American 15th MEU. The attack was an airmobile insertion that went well despite appalling weather, but plans to land Royal Marine light armored vehicles by hovercraft were abandoned at the last minute. The Royal Marines nevertheless pressed north, clearing the island without major resistance.

In the confusion of modern political, quasi-religious, and ethnic conflicts the forward-deployed American Marine MEUs find themselves tasked with a new variety of missions, including not only protection of lives and property. With the rise of religious separatist movements, a major task is now training local friendly government forces.

EPILOGUE

"It is the customary fate of new truths to begin as heresies and to end as superstitions."

Thomas Henry Huxley

Like some cinematic monster that keeps rising from the dead, amphibious warfare has repeatedly been declared obsolete, only to magically arise again so many times that it has become a cliché. The fact is that as a method of power projection, amphibious warfare is and will remain the only possibility. It is a matter of simple physics; outside the realm of science fiction, no other means exists of effectively transporting and maintaining major fighting forces over vast distances. The development of new equipment like heavy-lift helicopters and the American V-22 Osprey aircraft, both with air-to-air refueling capability, now allow amphibious force projection even into previously inaccessible areas like Afghanistan.

For many decades the United States has maintained supremacy as a practitioner of amphibious warfare. That is a matter of geography. As a major power bordered by two of the world's three major oceans, and with free access to each, it finds itself of necessity a major naval power, with the requirement for a strong amphibious capability.

Since World War II the amphibious capabilities of major powers have waxed and waned. Today most Western nations have increased their amphibious capability to at least a minimal degree, with countries like France, Italy, Australia and others possessing various capabilities. Britain in particular learned a harsh lesson in the near-disaster that was the Falklands War. Even strictly local

The American heavy Landing Craft, Utility (LCU), a heavy landing craft little-changed since World War II, is capable of carrying much heavier modern Main Battle Tanks. This LCU is depositing a South Korean K1 main battle tank on the beach during a recent exercise. (National Archives)

The helicopter revolutionized amphibious landings. Here a CH-46E troop carrier maneuvers above the beach, while below an LCAC disgorges eight-wheeled Light Armored Vehicles of a divisional Light Armored Reconnaissance Battalion. (National Archives)

Most equipment of the Russian Naval Infantry has very limited amphibious capability. The Alligator class Tank Landing Ship is designed to deposit vehicles directly onto the beach. Note that large bow doors. (US Navy)

powers as diverse as Thailand and Colombia maintain some limited amphibious capability; it is just too useful.

But two other major powers are rising to challenge American supremacy. Since the era of the tsars it has been a Russian ambition to achieve open access to the great oceans necessary to be a true global player. Since the resurrection of post-Soviet Russia the country has dramatically increased its fleet of smaller amphibious craft suitable for operations in the Baltic and Black seas. But the proposed construction of a large Lavinia-class amphibious assault ship roughly comparable to the older American Tarawa-class vessels remains controversial within Russia. The fact is that whatever its increasing emphasis on naval and amphibious capabilities, Russia remains bottled up by geography. Despite the establishment of new naval bases like Tartus, in Syria, it cannot force open and maintain free passage through the Bosporus, Danish Straits, or even the approaches to Vladivostok against any remotely credible air and sea power.

The main contender to American hegemony is the People's Republic of China. With a lengthy coastline that offers access to the East and South China seas, China possesses greater potential access to the open oceans, and quietly continues to grow its amphibious capabilities without much attention from the Western public. Most attention is devoted to Chinese island base construction in the South China Sea. Far less is devoted to the realization that China now has two amphibious mechanized divisions, an amphibious armored brigade, and two specialized Marine brigades, supported by over 30 modern tank landing ships, medium landing ships, and is acquiring assault hovercraft comparable to the American LCACs. The first thoroughly modern Yuzhao-class Landing Platform Dock was launched in January 2018, with more under construction, as well as a pair of modern Yuting II-class tank landing ships. In addition to conventional main battle tanks that can be carried by the new vessels, China has developed the ZTD-05 amphibious tank, now the world's fastest amphibious vehicle, with a 105mm cannon that fires both conventional rounds and guided missiles. Companion troop carriers with comparable capabilities are under development.

So despite all arguments to the contrary, amphibious warfare is not dead. It has only morphed into new forms in new and potentially more dangerous arenas.

FURTHER READING

There are numerous books on the history and theory of amphibious warfare, but the vast majority are subject-specific and cover certain battles, hardware and equipment, or influential individuals. In addition there is an enormous body of work included in military professional journals, historical journals, and other similar sources.

Four primary and readily available source books are:

- Bartlett, Merrill L. (editor), *Assault from the Sea: Essays on the History of Amphibious Warfare*, Naval Institute Press, Annapolis, 1993—an excellent collection of essays by subject matter experts, covering the ancient through modern eras.
- Daugherty, Leo J., *Pioneers of Amphibious Warfare, 1898–1945: Profiles of Fourteen American Military Strategists*, McFarland, Jefferson NC, 2009—biographies of the visionaries who developed modern amphibious doctrine.
- Isely, Jeter A., and Philip A. Crowl, *The U. S. Marines And Amphibious War: Its Theory and Practice in the Pacific*, Princeton University Press, Princeton NJ, 1951—a definitive and detailed academic study covering the development of modern doctrine and its application in the Pacific Theater. Unlike most studies, Isely and Crowl covered not only tactics and battle histories, but the nuts and bolts of amphibious warfare.
- Lovering, Tristan (editor), *Amphibious Assault: Maneouvre from the Sea*, Sheridan House, Lanham MD, 2007—a more up-to-date collection, covering more obscure subject matter.

INDEX